Born in Värnamo, Sweden, the Rev. G. Erik Hagg came to the United States at the age of 20, living at first in New England. After three years, having been guided and urged by the late Rev. Arvid J. Vikman, he enrolled at Luther Junior College, Wahoo, Nebraska, graduating in 1935. His college work was completed at Gustavus Adolphus College in 1936, and in 1940 he graduated from Augustana Seminary. Ordained in 1940, he served churches in Waltham, Massachusetts, and Batavia, Illinois, before coming to his present congregation, Faith Lutheran Church, Moline, Illinois, in 1954.

Pastor Hagg is in great demand as speaker and Bible teacher. He has written two quarters of the *Augustana Bible Study Quarterly* for 1958. He has served on several boards of his church, and is at present a member of the Board of Directors of Augustana Book Concern, and chairman of the Illinois Conference Commission on Social Problems.

PASSION PERSPECTIVES

Passion Perspectives

Sermons for Lent

By

G. ERIK HAGG

Pastor of Faith Lutheran Church

Moline, Illinois

AUGUSTANA PRESS

ROCK ISLAND, ILLINOIS

PASSION PERSPECTIVES

The Scripture passages in this publication, unless otherwise indicated, are from The Revised Standard Version of the Bible, copyright 1946 and 1952 by the Division of Christian Education, National Council of Churches of Christ in the United States of America, and are used by permission.

[PRINTED IN U·S·A·]

AUGUSTANA BOOK CONCERN

Printers and Binders

ROCK ISLAND, ILLINOIS

1958

To the memory

of my wife

JENNIE

whose life bore witness

to the redeeming power

of Christ's passion, death, and resurrection

better than my words can do

Contents

Foreword

REPEATED REQUESTS from friends, throughout the years, that I publish some of my sermons and "see what will happen" are partly responsible for this my first attempt at preaching through "the printed word." Since all of the ten discourses were preached during the 1957 Lenten season in Faith Lutheran Church, Moline, I am more grateful than my words can possibly convey to members and friends of Faith, including seminary, college, and school of nursing students, for their kind and encouraging response. When young people of college and seminary standing joined with the members and friends of a young congregation (Faith is only 7 years old) and gave the "go ahead" signal, this preacher could do no less than agonize and organize the inspiration and information given him until they took the form and shape of "Passion Perspectives."

Moreover, there came additional encouragement from the Augustana Book Concern when I was asked to prepare a series of sermons for the 1958 Lenten Season. Naturally, I felt both flattered and flattened by such an invitation, and there seemed little else to do but to write my visions, impressions, and interpretations of our Lord's passion, death, and resurrection into a book. Inasmuch as the composition and delivery of these messages coincided with my own personal passion experience, suffered in the passing of my wife on February 9, 1957, I seemed to gain and attain perspectives never known to me before. I cannot explain how, but it was and is the realest, truest experience in my life, that though dead she still speaks, and inspires my meditation and thinking. No doubt, from the heights where she now dwells there are "perspectives" no man has seen. Yet glimpses escape into the minds and land of the living.

Dr. Victor E. Beck has aided and assisted me in ways too numerous to itemize here. Suffice it to say that he has my sincere gratitude and admiration for patience and understanding. I have no secretary, but no professional stenographer could have done a better job in deciphering and typing my illegible scribbling than Mrs. Francis Ford, a member of Faith Church. To her, and to hosts of others, I shall be indebted always for time and talents spent so generously in my behalf.

Needless to say that since I yielded to the urgings that I publish some of my sermons, I am anticipating somewhat anxiously "what will happen," if anything. Whatever the outcome, I know in advance that in writing a book, as in everything else, "It is more blessed to give than to receive."

I send forth this my first printed sample of homiletical workmanship in the hope that it shall be the means of making plainer the great and often uninhabited regions of "Passion Perspectives."

Faith Lutheran Parsonage
Moline, Illinois

G. ERIK HAGG

From that time Jesus began to show his disciples that he must go to Jerusalem and suffer many things from the elders and chief priests and scribes, and be killed.

Matthew 16:21

When the days drew near for him to be received up, he set his face to go to Jerusalem.

Luke 9:51

The Two Roads

ONE OF OUR Lord's most familiar admonitions is the one in which He urges His followers to "enter in at the strait gate: for wide is the gate, and broad is the way, that leadeth to destruction, and many there be which go in thereat: Because strait is the gate, and narrow is the way, which leadeth unto life, and few there be that find it." (K.J.V.)

In other words, "the two roads," destruction and life, are in these vivid word pictures suddenly flashed before our eyes, and through them we can see some facts about life that cannot be gainsaid or reasoned away. Inasmuch as this passage or parable is not one of the traditional Ash Wednesday texts, it has the additional advantage that the truth set forth is for year round, even lifelong application. He who loves life, and desires to enter into the good land, must not only follow a particular road, but must also pass through a particular gate.

It is at this point that the carefree attitude of the worldly wise becomes both fallacious and fatal, when he says that the roads "are many and different, but they terminate or converge at the same place." Note carefully that nothing is said about the roads coming to an absolute and inevitable stop at "the narrow gate." The Christian religion boldly declares that the man who roams and wanders everywhere may never discover where the road takes him, and may never arrive at the goal of life, for "strait is the gate." By the same token, he who is in earnest pursuit of the strait gate must follow the narorw way that leads there.

Of a truth, it is easier and surely much more pleasant, even for those of us who cannot carry a tune, to sing, "Lift up our hearts, hear us, we pray, And lead us in life's narrow way," than it is to put the prayer into practice. As a matter of fact, "the strait and narrow" is not a very popular quotation among us, regardless of its Scriptural source and the renewed interest that religion is reported to enjoy in our society. Curiously enough, we can put up with the word "straight," especially if we are not told to make straight what long was "crooked," but the word "narrow" is out of favor altogether. We neither admire nor accept narrowness.

To be thought and considered narrow-minded is insulting and injurious to our good opinion of ourselves. The broad view of life has an irresistible appeal, even though it is often no more than a flattened expansion, completely vacant and devoid of all the spiritual furnishings which make life worth living. But if we believe in God, and in Him whom He sent, even Jesus Christ, then we must preach and practice the truth that narrowness is an essential part of life. Make no mistake about it, life has its narrow gates. There is no better time given us than the beginning of another Lenten season to meditate about the two roads that lead, one to destruction and one to life.

When I was a child and, like Paul, felt, thought, and spoke as a child, in my childish mind I divided the year into sections or parts. Ordinary, daily, and weekly activities occupied more than 360 days; sometimes they ran as high as 363. The two shining exceptions were the closing exercises in our little country schoolhouse, where six grades held forth under incredibly primitive conditions, and our annual Sunday school parade when, accompanied by a brass band and beating drums, we marched through the city in triumph. The faithful, dependable, and strong boys were selected to carry the flags displayed by each class. What a narrow path it was, and how straitened the way— as well as the shoulders of each flag-bearer. No room there for the jaywalker and the strayer from the beaten path. Straight as a ramrod was the carriage of the ones chosen to represent their class, and their outward appearance became a symbol of the inner spiritual rectitude of their lives. Much the same standards were applied in the country schoolhouse.

Life within its walls was rather uneventful, except when on the last day of school, in the presence of our parents and superiors, the diligent and studious were asked to come up to the front and recite before all the assembled dignitaries and guests. Again it was a narrow path that led up to the place of exaltation and recognition. Nevertheless, those two days still stand out in retrospect as more valuable than all the times we had played ball, or Indian war games, or "run, sheep, run," with virtually the whole broad countryside as our field of action.

Since those days of boyish exuberance I have walked a number of narrow paths, including the confirmation trail that led to the altar rail, where I made vows and promises involving my relationship with God and my fellow men. There has been the narrow aisle of matrimony, blessed in memory where, forsaking all others, the promise was made to love and cherish *one,* in prosperity as well as in adversity. Moreover there have been rather narrow passageways which at commencement time have taken me up to the platform where diplomas have been issued because I had consented to narrow myself down to certain prescribed courses, and had finished them according to the requirements laid down and enforced by educational experts.

Indeed, life's major goals are reached through shockingly and surprisingly narrow gates. Sometimes, when in a reminiscent mood, I think of the millions of people who have come to the United States of America by the way of Ellis Island. Since I am one of them, I can testify personally that the way is narrow and the gate is strait that leads to life in these United States. Undesirable aliens are not wanted, even though America is a land of unbelievable room. Despite the wide open spaces in America, there is no vacancy anywhere for those who plot the overthrow of the government by force. Obvious moral defects and handicaps, as well as mental reservations about giving United States full allegiance, are just too big risks even for a country the size of ours. But notwithstanding these necessary limitations, there is room in the hearts of Americans to welcome all other sorts and conditions of men who desire a larger, fuller, freer, and more abundant life. The asylum granted freedom fighters and political refugees, in addition to the material aid extended both at home and abroad, prove that life in America is incredibly large. However, the strait gate that opens into that larger way of life allows only those who are willing to adhere to time-honored decencies and dignities.

So it is with all of life. Scriptures speak of both valleys and gates of decision. As we view our lives in retrospect, we discover numerous gates through which we have passed. All of them are gates of decision, of destiny-making proportions. Some of them have had to do with our education, our life work, our friends, our life mates, our loyalties, and our attitudes.

Such decisions are made by all people, and many of them are within very definite limits and boundaries. With respect to the choice of parents and environment we may well argue with John Oxenham's frequently misapplied assertion,

> But to every soul there openeth
> A High Way and a Low.
> And every soul decideth
> The way he shall go.

Obviously enough, there are matters and circumstances over which we have little or no choice at all. But within recognized and established limits we are still free to make decisions. We must decide whether we want to live at the center of life, or whether we are satisfied to hover about its fringes. By the grace of God we need not be victims, but rather victors "in all the strife of mortal life." Each time we enter more deeply and devotedly into the constructive areas of life we do so by means of decision. We pass through a gate that is real enough to remind us of Ruskin's word of caution, "Remember if you read this book now, you cannot read that one." In reading books, as in rendering service, it is impossible to serve two masters simultaneously, nor does anyone have the know-how to travel the two roads, the one to life and the one to destruction, at one and the same time.

True enough, there are those who avoid a choice by postponing their decision. They do not choose to pass through some of the gates that lead into life. Little do they realize that their indecision is in itself a decision. We may procrastinate about making up our minds, but we cannot delay making up our lives. It does us no good whatever that we know our way around, if we never get on our way. Time and again we meet people who, though they live in the shadow of places and institutions freighted with historical and spiritual significance, never pass through the gate that admits them into the finer and better things of life. Vividly do I remember the profound impression Valley Forge made upon me when I visited it for the first time, and how shocked I was when less than fifty miles from this famous historical shrine I encountered a native-born Pennsylvanian who with ill-concealed pride in his ignorance declared, "I was born and raised here, but I have never been there."

The beginning of another Lenten season is a time when you and I are faced with gateways of decision in the most unique and challenging manner. On the one hand,

"There is a gate that stands ajar,
And through its portals gleaming,
A radiance from the cross afar,
The Saviour's love revealing."

The message of Lent is urgent, reminding us that mercy's gate is still open "for all who seek through it salvation, the rich and poor, the great and small, of every tribe and nation."

On the other hand, opposite to mercy's gate is the gateway of misery. In the words of Holy Writ, "There is a way which seems right to a man, but its end is the way to death." Centuries ago, when Jesus set His face steadfastly to go to Jerusalem, those that followed Him were sore afraid. Even some of His closest and most intimate disciples watched Him at a safe distance, and when the going became rougher than flesh and blood could endure, they all forsook Him and fled. One entered the gate of betrayal, another the gate of denial, and several sneaked through the broad way and the wide gate of cowardice and expediency. It was by such tactics and methods that the Prince of Life and Peace was killed originally, and similar procedures do crucify Him again here and now.

So the choice of life and death is before us! We can do our part to usher in the kind of life God intends His children to have in the world, a life in which men and women co-operate with each other for the purposes of peace and good will rather than compete with each other for the purposes of profit and ultimately of war. A gateway of decision stands open into a land of racial equality, international justice, peace on earth, and good will toward men.

There is nothing that says we must make the decision to abolish war and make the blessings of God available to all men everywhere. It may be that we shall decide to forfeit the opportunity. The sufferings of the present time may leave us completely cold and indifferent, as we rush by on the other side of the wide, wide world's busy thoroughfares. Certain it is that prophets and wise men have desired and prayed for like opportunities, and have neither seen nor possessed them. The broad road of earthly pleasure and gain may look alluring at present, but it narrows until it finally ends in chains and slavery. True deliverance is found only in the narrow way that broadens into eternal life and liberty.

Today is the day of salvation. Gateways of opportunity are before us, and I pray that we may have both the courage and the vision to go through the gates, proclaiming as we go along " 'Behold, your salvation comes; behold, his reward is with him, and his recompense before him.' And they shall be called The holy people, The redeemed of the Lord; and you shall be called Sought out, a city not forsaken." The clear and unmistakable light that was never seen on land and sea marks the road that leads us to the Lamb that takes away the sins of the world.

How important our choice is for both the here and the hereafter is indicated in the stanza:

I shall be telling this with a sigh,
Somewhere ages and ages hence
Two roads diverged in the woods, and I—
Took the one less traveled by
And that has made all the difference.[1]

[1] From Mountain Interval by Robert Frost. By permission of the publishers, Henry Holt and Company. Copyright 1916, 1921 and by Robert Frost 1944.

The Two Reeds

REEDS GROW EVERYWHERE in Palestine so I am told. They range from six to fifteen feet in height, and have commercial as well as cultural value in the manufacturing of musical instruments, paper, and pens. In olden times reeds were also used as measuring rods, a fact mentioned in both the Old and the New Testaments. Most of the time, however, the sacred writers refer to the reed as a symbol of weakness and fragility.

Thus the prophet Ahijah delivers God's judgments against Jeroboam's house saying "The Lord will smite Israel, as a reed is shaken in the water." Foreign alliances and connivings with Egypt, which have a familiar and up-to-date relevance right now, are denounced in no uncertain terms in 2 Kings: "Behold, you are relying now on Egypt, that broken reed of a staff, which will pierce the hand of any man who leans on it. Such is Pharaoh king of Egypt to all who rely on him."

Ezekiel returns repeatedly to the same theme of gloom and doom for Egypt, "Because you have been a staff of reed to the house of Israel." Isaiah concurs by predicting that the downfall of Egypt shall be so complete that even "the reeds and rushes will rot away," but concerning the kindness of Messiah, the Suffering Servant, the prophet predicts that "a bruised reed he will not break."

Other well-known incidents, involving reeds, include the hiding and finding of Moses "among the reeds at the river's brink," and our Lord's question concerning John the Baptist, "What did you go out into the wilderness to behold? A reed shaken by the wind?"

While it is obvious that these questions of Jesus convey the picture of what John was not, they also give us a rather vivid image of the reed as a symbol of compliance. For one thing, it is a plant that adapts itself to conditions as they are. No one expects this kin of the grass family to have a will or mind of its own. As you will, sir, or as you please, madam, has been the disposition of the reed from time immemorial, and it is still the same today. Like too many people we know, the reed is willing to be used as means to an end rather than as an end in itself. The importance of Immanuel Kant's insistence that no man should be used as a tool in the hands of another mortal, but that each person is created in the image of God as an end in himself, is illustrated with matchless clarity in the role played by the reed wielders in the trial and crucifixion of our Lord. Men are ends, not eggs for Napoleonic omelets, or pawns for a social or recreational or even spiritual program.

Unforgettable, indeed, is the graphic manner in which Matthew and Mark relate how, when the soldiers had platted a crown of thorns, they put it upon our Savior's head, and a reed in His right hand and bowed the knee before Him and mocking Him, saying, "Hail, King of the Jews!" Then they spit upon Him, and took the reed and smote Him upon the head.

In this instance the ever pliable reed became an instrument of injury and derision. For the first and only time in history, God surrendered himself into the hands of sinful men, saying in effect, "Do with me whatsoever you will. I am yours. Whether you choose to crown or crucify me, to treat me as king or criminal, is entirely within your power." Sad to say, there was a substantial majority in both church and state who felt that, since this was their hour, they would make the most of it by dethroning Him and trimming Him down in size until He was a non-entity, a sorry spectacle, a sad mixture of king and clown.

So they staged a mock coronation; the reed would be His royal scepter. But it could also be used as a whip or club, a channel through which they communicated their contempt of the holy and their own lack of decency and self-respect. It seemed such a funny thing to do, but what a perverted sense of humor it turned out to be! As has happened so many times since, the foolishness of God was wiser than the wisdom of men, and the weakness of God was stronger than the might of men.

For though the soldiers raged so furiously together, and though the people were satisfied momentarily that they had "no king but Caesar," and though the tortured body of Jesus turned and twisted until it became a veritable question mark, "My God, my God why hast thou forsaken me?" the reed wielded by a man of mercy vouchsafed pity in the most distressing and dreadful moment the world has ever known. As usual there was much talking and speculating as to what would be the next move, or who would make it.

Some ventured the guess that perhaps Elijah would come, or there would be the manifestation of supernatural powers. There was only one man of action, and the Evangelists relate what he did without fanfare or a flare for the dramatic. Yet their reporting is such that the world has never been able to forget it. "And one ran and, filling a sponge full of vinegar, and put it on a reed and gave him to drink." In this instance the reed became the channel of helpfulness, kindness, and consideration. The reed need not sway in the wind, nor need it participate in acts of cruelty and mockery.

By the same token individuals need not go along with every stormy wind that blows; they can oppose and go contrary to even the fiercest crosscurrents of wind and wave. That unknown hero who on the first Good Friday made himself immortal, though nameless, still speaks through his deed of kindness and act of love that life belongs to those who, under God, master it rather than are mastered by it. The lowly reed in dedicated hands may yet perform service, for in the words of a familiar stewardship hymn,

> Nothing so small can be
> But draws, when acted for Thy sake,
> Greatness and worth from Thee.

Now let us consider for a moment that the difference between the reed of helpfulness and the reed of harmfulness is not in the reeds themselves. Perhaps they grew side by side. It may be that they were identical twins in the reed family. Those who passed by the place where they grew and developed could never have predicted in advance that the one would become an instrument of torture while the other would acquire renown as a carrier of comfort in the hour of grief and pain.

The great difference between the two reeds must, therefore, be attributed to the people who used them. Still further, the distinction must be traced to the imagination of those who looked upon the two reeds, and started to dream dreams and see visions of their future usefulness. The soldiers saw in the reed an instrument useful for their plans to conquer both the bodies and minds of men. Sad to say, the urge to use God's gifts to kill and frighten the defenseless and the weak has not changed, except for the worse. It is even more true today than it was when God first observed in the days of Noah that "the wickedness of man was great in the earth, and that every imagination of the thoughts of his heart was only evil continually. And the Lord was sorry that he had made man on the earth, and it grieved him to his heart."

The fighting, feuding, and fussing side of man's nature still regards every new discovery of science as another opportunity to get power while getting is good, and to speak gruffly and threateningly while carrying the big stick of dynamite or nuclear missiles. The most accurate description of power-possessed and still power-hungry humanity is the brief sketch of a character in a recent novel to the effect that, "his servility was so boisterous that it looked like independence." In other words, we are not using all the power entrusted to us, but rather it is using us. The soldiers were not using the reed as much as they were used by it. Instead of being conquerors they were the vanquished, and their act was merely an empty show of strength that deluded and deceived no one but themselves. This was well expressed in unhappy Hungary recently where two ladies reportedly told Russian soldiers, "You have guns and you have fears. We have no guns and no fears." And One greater than they said long ago in connection with His own arrest, "All who take the sword will perish by the sword."

When drunk with military might and power, as most of the world seems to be at the moment, and when on state and gala occasions we let loose verbal blasts and gun salutes to frighten our foes and slay their confidence, it seems both safe and sane to ask, "Are we making anybody besides ourselves fear and tremble at the sight and cost of all this potential arsenal of destruction and death?"

Somewhere in the United States there is reported to be an inscription on a railroad station which reads, "Strength is not in the majority but in the sincerity of the will to sacrifice."

The solo performance in the drama of Calvary, when one man took a reed to minister to the dying Savior of the world, illustrates perfectly the sincerity of this man's will to sacrifice and serve both his God and neighbor. Even such a little, plain and simple thing as a reed can be used to accomplish great and never-to-be forgotten benefits.

Were we to interview this kindly, human soul, and inquire into the motives which prompted him to love this strange man on the cross, when even God appeared to have forsaken Him, and most of His friends had fled, the reason given would no doubt be: "I put myself in His place." Such an attitude calls for a greater measure of imagination, kindliness, and discipline of spirit, than most of us are willing either to cultivate or utilize. This is the Golden Rule in action. "Whatever you wish that men would do to you, do so to them; for this is the law and the prophets." There is nothing more impressive in the prophet Ezekiel's autobiography than his terse and matter-of-fact statement, "I sat where they sat." One there was who could not see the loneliness and despair of his fellow citizens in exile and remain aloof and unmoved by their plight. Ezekiel had to share their woes, even as centuries later the man with the reed identified himself with Him concerning whom it had been foretold that "he will not break a bruised reed." Throughout His life Jesus put himeslf so definitely in the place of needy humanity that Paul later wrote that "he (God) made him to be sin who knew no sin," and again that, "though he was rich, yet for your sake he became poor, so that by his poverty you might become rich."

It is said that the only true artist and author is the one who puts himself in the place of his characters. What painters and poets do for art, Jesus does for life. He understands the longings and the remorse of the prodigal son, and He suffers with the woman of Samaria, even before she herself realized the depths of her own misery. He identifies himself with the grief-stricken widow of Nain in such a way as to make mourners everywhere feel, "Surely he has borne our griefs and carried our sorrows."

Dealing with a hated taxgatherer, a social outcast named Zacheaus, he dined at his house. To an erring woman he said, "Neither do I condemn you; go, and do not sin again." Since a disciple is not above his master, or a servant greater than his Lord, it becomes imperative that "we should follow in his steps" in much the same manner as the good man did who had only a pliable reed at his disposal.

The truth of the matter is that we are called and expected to do likewise. Let us suppose for a moment that employers and employees could or would take ten minutes each day to think of one another's problems. Moreover, let us imagine that parents and children would spend some time each day thinking of what they would do if the shoe were on the other foot. Suppose still further that Jews and Gentiles would exchange position and habits of thinking until they were concerned about other ethnic groups as well as their own. Problems of race and commerce, politics and industry, religion and education are solved more readily by the reed that heals than by the reed that smites. Only by goodness will evil ever be vanquished.

These things are so self-evident that I would not mention them at all, were it not for the fact that there is more need for the gentle, healing reed than ever before in history. There are times when we ask impatiently, "How long, O Lord? How long shall we have to bear with these exasperating people and conditions?" Even our Lord asked that question once.

All we have to do is to picture ourselves as a hungry pair of hands reaching for bread, or as in the place of those who have no language but a cry that tells of pain and suffering, or as being part of the multitude that lives in the twilight of superstition and ignorance, and we will be constrained to use all that we have, even if it be only a reed, to minister in the name of Him who said, "As you did it to one of the least of these my brethren, you did it to me."

The Two Robbers

ONLY A FEW of the Passion characters are known to us by name. Still fewer are known to us by virtue of their position and disposition. Among them are such ecclesiastical renegades as Annas and Caiaphas. The best and most charitable statement we can make about the faith practiced by the religious leaders who advocated the death of Jesus is our Lord's own statement that "they say and do not."

Then there is Herod the king, whose conduct was so far from kingly, and at whose bidding so many lives were snuffed out prematurely, that he becomes what the poet calls, "Familiar as an old mistake and futile as regret."

Much the same can be said about Pilate, the Roman governor, who lives and lingers on in the hall of infamy because Jesus was "crucified under Pontius Pilate." He illustrates well what has become a proverbial saying among us, "There is no rest for the wicked."

Joseph of Arimathea is remembered because he was such a strange mixture of faith and fear. "A disciple of Jesus, but secretly, for fear of the Jews, (he) asked Pilate that he might take away the body of Jesus, and Pilate gave him leave."

"Nicodemus also, who had at the first come to him by night, came bringing a mixture of myrrh and aloes, about a hundred pounds' weight. They took the body of Jesus, and bound it in linen cloths with the spices, as is the burial custom of the Jews."

To hear and see fear give way to faith is always an enriching experience. How we wish that the report concerning the twelve apostles and their part in our Lord's Passion had a better ending than the tragic "they all forsook him, and fled." Judas went out into the night to betray Him, while Peter denied Him. John, the beloved disciple, was probably rescued "from despair, and other great and shameful sins," by Mary, the mother of Jesus. At any rate, Mary and John were at the cross when the third word from that strange pulpit was spoken by Jesus, "Woman, behold your Son!" "Behold your mother!"

Simon of Cyrene, the drafted cross-bearer, just about completes the list of named and known characters who, in one way or another, had a part in the suffering and death of our Lord. Altogether there are only a score of people whose names and deeds are identified and connected with the last and final movements and moments of our Lord's life before He suffered, died, and was buried.

With only some twenty characters known even to Bible students, there is reason to conclude that most of the participants in the drama of Calvary are unknown entities, concerning whom it must be said that they are "known but to God." The people in the crowd are in that category. We know neither how many nor who they were. It is rather certain, however, that there was an impressive number from all walks of life who demanded that Jesus be put to death.

Even the two robbers who were crucified with Jesus are nameless individuals, though traditions and legends have given them the names of Dismas and Gestas. Scriptures tells us nothing about their names or ancestry. Their only reason for remembrance by posterity is that one was crucified on the left and the other on the right side of Jesus.

So it is only natural that we should wonder and ask how they got started on their careers of crime and violence. Much and helpful information could be gained if we knew something about their family backgrounds. Did they come from good homes? Were their families unsuspecting and unaware about the activities of their sons? Had they succeeded completely in pulling the wool over the eyes of their loved ones? Could it be that they were the original and genuine Dr. Jekyll and Mr. Hyde?

Are their names withheld because of a desire to protect the families involved, or did they come from the wrong side of the tracks, where they were numbered among the nobodies, concerning whom names and titles reveal nothing in particular anyway? Had they been pampered from early childhood, or had they been ill-treated and maligned as far back as they could remember? These and many other questions come to mind wherever and whenever the two robbers between whom Jesus died come up for review and reappraisal. This is true especially in our own day and age when both heredity and environment are regarded as destiny-making factors of major importance. We can only guess and speculate as to the influences which kept pushing them relentlessly in the direction of a green hill far away, where they gained lasting remembrance because Jesus was between them.

Come to think about it, Jesus is between every one of us and nothingness. Without Christ and without hope in the world, we are not only miserable, but also wretchedly deficient; for apart from Him "all that pleases is valueless on earth." It is only when Jesus stands between us and extinction that we can shout defiantly, "Death is swallowed up in victory." With Him as our mediator, we are assured that dust is not our destiny. If it were not so, He would have told us.

However, before we proceed further in our attempt to find the causes that led the robbers to their cruel death, we need to remind ourselves that the descent to the lower life is easy, and the enticements are many. The poet's warning words are, therefore, both timely and timeless:

> Judge not hastily the brother
> Who from virtue's path has strayed
> For you have not weighed the burden
> Fate upon his shoulders laid;
> And you do not know the struggles
> He maintained in virtue's name;
> Neither do you know the anguish
> Which he suffers for his shame.

Moreover, what Robert Frost, the poet said on the television program "Meet the press" on December 23, 1956, deserves special consideration and emphasis, "One thing that will never change. It will always be costly to save the soul to preserve decency."

Society has been slow to recognize this inescapable truth. In spite of almost 2,000 years of Christian teaching and preaching, our homes and communities, and churches too, leave undone their essential assignment, and concentrate all the more feverishly on the trivial. Our best efforts are concentrated upon things that belong to war rather than upon the qualities that belong to peace. The words Jesus spoke when He wept over Jerusalem are as relevant today as they were then, "Would that even today you knew the things that make for peace! But now they are hid from your eyes."

Without straining or taxing our imagination at all, we may venture the opinion that it is very possible that the two robbers had served in the army. There they had been taught to engage in guerilla warfare against the Romans. Thus they antedate by some twenty centuries today's "freedom fighters." Bloodshed had become an indispensable item in their daily life and diet. There is nothing wrong, of course, in fighting for home, country, and freedom; but there is something inherently wrong in a world order that encourages the "go getters," no matter where they go or what they get.

To make murder and killing a normal and expected routine, where the shedding of blood is part of the day's work, is sin whether it happens in first-century Palestine or in twentieth-century America, Asia, or Europe. The standard of the infinite worth of each child of God is raised over the body of each needlessly sacrificed person in judgment on a civilization which would rather sacrifice its sons than abandon its hatreds, its fears, its prejudices, and its lust for power.

What Marshal Haig is reported to have said at the close of the first World War is a goal as yet unattained, "It is the business of the church to stop the bloody business of war." This will not be done by spending most of our money and intellect in the service of the god of war, and forgetting all about the Prince of Peace. Mouthing pious slogans affords no lasting peace of mind or peace on earth.

That a mother and father who give their sons to the armed services as military sacrifices are singled out for recognition and reward, while parents who give their sons to peaceful pursuits in all the various walks of life are seldom or never mentioned, is but another example of our perverted sense of values. The man who kills in the line of duty is decorated, but if he does the same while on leave from the services, he is condemned and often sentenced to death. When he spies on the enemy, he is in the intelligence service, but when caught by the enemy in the act of clandestinely or on false pretenses seeking information with the intent of reporting it to his superiors, he is summarily sentenced to death. It may be that, if the facts were known, Dismas and Gestas could tell us quite a story about how immoral society can and does ruin good morals more often than not.

Anyway the two robbers were companions in lawlessness in a day when, as now, human flesh was cheap. They were comrades in the misfortune that nearly always befalls those who take the law into their own hands in that they were arrested, tried, and sentenced to pay the penalty. Together they were condemned, and together they carried their crosses to a hill far away. When they arrived they were crucified in that methodical, thoroughgoing manner which was typical of Rome's conception of order and justice. They had been caught red-handed in the very act of rebellion, and Rome said that they would have to die.

However, at the approach of death the similarity between the two robbers ends abruptly and decisively. We are told that the one malefactor railed on our blessed Lord, saying, "Are you not the Christ? Save yourself and us." His soul was hardened and impervious to any gentle, kind, or helpful influence. He chose to die as he had lived, consistently defiant to the very end. With his head bloody but unbowed, he went down with his flag flying, a perfect example of the infamous rebel cry:

"It matters not how strait the gate,
How charged with punishment the scroll,
I am the master of my fate;
I am the captain of my soul."

But because of his boastful attitude and defiance of God, the tide of death carried him far and beyond the island of safety and the shore of redemption. Rebellion against God always is a losing proposition. To make trial and mockery of the Eternal is bound to end in irreparable failure and never-ending tragedy.

But the second robber was so different that when he heard his fellow partner in crime assail Jesus, he rebuked him saying, "Do you not fear God, since you are under the same sentence of condemnation? And we indeed justly; for we are receiving the due reward of our deeds; but this man has done nothing wrong." And he said, "Jesus, remember me when you come into your kingly power." Then Jesus answered him, "Truly, I say to you, today you will be with me in Paradise."

Here is a man who is trying to lead his rebellious fellow sufferer to the mourner's bench, in order that help might be vouchsafed him in this dire hour of need. Having done that, he places himself before the mercy seat, asking only that he might be remembered. And lo, from his misery we see him rise to a home in Paradise.

It is not necessary for us to read into this remarkable confession and prayer any specific brand of either theology or philosophy. All we need to remember is that the man is crying out of the depths of his soul. At heart he is an intensely sensitive, even decent sort of chap. A victim of a whole chain of unfavorable circumstances, he is more sinned against than sinning. He sees in Jesus the helper of the helpless and asks that where the Savior of the world is, there he might be also.

This is, therefore, the place where we must take issue with those who maintain that the same thing happened to both of them. True enough, both died, and when they had breathed their last, the one was as dead as the other. Death is no respecter of person. The good often dies at a younger age than the wicked, which may have been true here also. Be that as it may, soberly and unescapably death comes to all men. But the determining factor is not the external event, but our preparation for it and our reaction to it. One uses the name of God in vain, the other uses it in prayer, confession, and adoration. From the lips of the impenitent robber comes the blasphemous question, "What kind of man is this Jesus who will not use His heavenly prerogatives to free His fellow sufferers?" while the other acknowledges the royal visage and bearing of Jesus as a guarantee that He will make death glorious and triumphant.

The impenitent thief deplores the fact that murder will out, while the penitent one implores Jesus to let the murderer in from the fields of sin. In the one case Paradise lost is an irretrievable fact, not even God can swing wide its gates, but in the other the emphasis is upon Paradise regained. We live in a world where it is possible to be lost, but where it is also possible to be found. No one needs to stay the way he is or where he is. Whosoever draws near God will discover God already near to him, even as the prodigal son found the father waiting and the penitent thief found Jesus ready to welcome, pardon, cleanse, relieve,

"And to mortals
Opening the heavenly portals."

So the story of the two robbers tells us how they died upon Calvary within speaking distance of the Son of Man, "who died to save us all." One prayed, and was saved. Clear as the sound of silver bells came the answer that very day, not in the sweet by and by, but that day before the sun set, he would be with the Savior in Paradise.

Salvation and the eternal mansions were only a prayer away. The other did not pray and, suffered the sentence of condemnation, both here and hereafter. However, for the repentant soul, there is life and there is hope. Regardless of how many our failures and shortcomings are, the promise remains:

"There is welcome for the sinner,
And more graces for the good;
There is mercy with the Saviour;
There is healing in His blood.

"For the love of God is broader
Than the measure of man's mind;
And the heart of the Eternal
Is most wonderfully kind."

The Two Robes

IRONICAL INCIDENTS ABOUND in the trial and condemnation of Jesus in the court of Pilate. The Roman governor himself is responsible for that choice sample of irony which appeared in the form of a written title on the cross, "Jesus of Nazareth, King of the Jews."

Doubtless the chief object of Pilate in composing such an inscription was to wreak vengeance upon the Jews. They had succeeded in their mad scheme to send Jesus to His death only because Pilate had allowed himself to become their servant. This humiliated and galled Pilate no end. As a final act of defiance and empty show of independence, he would poison, if he could, the cup of triumph of scribe and Pharisee. It may even be that he was glad thus to indicate his own estimate of Christ's superiority.

If so, he was a great success, as is evidenced rather clearly in the corrective measures the chief priests demanded, "Do not write, 'The King of the Jews,' but, 'This man said, I am King of the Jews.' " Pilate's only comment was, "What I have written I have written."

Then there is the irony-laden event, planned and put into operation by the soldiers who mocked, beat, and blindfolded Jesus to the tune of "Prophesy to us, you Christ! Who is it that struck you?"

To add insult to injury, they gave Him a reed for a scepter

and thorns for a crown. Mark and John tell us that they provided Him with a purple robe; Luke says it was gorgeous, and Matthew describes it as scarlet. But all the Evangelists were so impressed by the irony of the arrangement that they include the robe as an article they remembered and felt worth preserving in their account of our Lord's passion and death.

It certainly is passing strange that He who cared not at all for the external and outward symbols of kingliness was to be clothed and classed as king. Repeatedly He told all who had ears to hear that His kingdom was not of this world. The response of many was to number Him among transgressors, and to treat Him with mock gravity. The extravagant images and incongruous contrasts, created to excite laughter and contempt, stand out in still sharper relief when we remember that Jesus was reluctant even about being called Messiah because of the political implications involved. In the accepted and expected terminology and pattern of the world, Jesus was neither a king nor the Messiah whom they awaited to slay their foes and lift them high.

So when He didn't conform or accommodate himself to their standards, they retaliated by making Him appear outlandish, ridiculous, and burlesque. Yet, He endured all these gainsayings from sinners, and accepted all this travesty upon justice, in the firm conviction that it is better to be faithful to God than famous with men; better to be righteous in the sight of the heavenly Father than royal in the eyes of men, who see only the outward appearance and pay no attention to the heart; better to be kindly affectioned even to evildoers than kingly, if that means the exercising of external authority and a haughty attitude toward people. Let the world deride or pity, but as for Jesus, "the cup that my Father has given me shall I not drink it?" was at the beginning and ending of all His actions.

Amidst the manifold changes and cares of life He still insists that we should take a chance with God now. It is a queer thing about life that he who is willing to settle for anything but God's best is bound to get it, and when he gets it he is most miserable. Only in God and on God's terms is the best for us obtainable and available. We have to receive Him the way He comes to us, and register no protest if and when He comes in a manner or form different from our blueprints or notions about Him.

This word of caution and warning applies to us as well as to the contemporaries of Jesus. Perhaps it should be stated right here that we ought not imitate those who robed Jesus according to their own imagined needs, something that we do more often than we may be willing to admit. As a matter of fact, what the soldiers did is what men have been doing since that day until now. We dress Jesus according to our own fashion fads. Labor is prone to think of Him as a man in overalls, a carpenter who has paid his union dues, or as the slogan put it years ago by those who were out to convert the working man, "Comrade Jesus has paid his dues." Of course, He has and besides, He is a friend of all "who labor and are heavy-laden." That includes employers also, and so you have Bruce Barton writing a whole book titled *The Man Nobody Knows.* In it Jesus is pictured as a highly successful business man, whose ruthless and "go getter" tactics made Him the envy of all who measure success in terms of money and fame gained in business transactions.

For those who labor and are heavy-laden with concerns about getting rich quick, regardless of the means employed, Jesus would undoubtedly still offer the rest from earthly cares which comes from following Him. He did that to the rich young ruler once, and there is every reason to believe that His message would be the same today. To make Jesus wear a business man's suit only will be as difficult as limiting Him to overalls or the robe of militarism. That, too, has been tried with varying degrees of success. Even passion and vindictiveness have taken cover behind a uniform designed to fight for God and country. Earth and land and sea still contain a plentiful and pitiful supply of what remains from those millions upon millions of young lives who went out killing and being killed, maiming and being maimed, because it was "the will of God." Although the last war had relatively few slogans that in the name of God incited and invited violence, we still remember, "God on the battle wagon" and "Praise the Lord and pass the ammunition." Such catch words as "Remember Pearl Harbor," and the much older "Remember the Maine," should be replaced by "Remember Jesus Christ," of which reminder they are such tragic perversions.

Theologians and men of thought have been busy trying to dress up our Lord and harness Him with all kinds of holy millinery. There is the intriguing texture of philosophical weaving. Certainly thought enters into our most holy faith, and conversely it should and must enter into all that we say, think, or do. Reason has its place, "Come now, let us reason together, says the Lord." Moreover, we ought to be able to give a reason for the faith that is in us. Yet when all is said and done Luther's reminder is apropos that we cannot by our own reason or strength believe in Jesus Christ or come to Him, but "the Holy Spirit has called (us) through the gospel, enlightened (us) by His gifts, and sanctified and preserved (us) in the true faith." Then, too, as Pascal reminds us, "The heart has its reasons, which reason does not understand."

Additional robes prepared for Jesus by overzealous reformers and ritualists include the extreme emphasis upon forms and postures, ceremony and clerical garbs and vestments, until the idea is created that the Word has become garments and mere attire, rather than flesh and personality in whom and through whom God speaks and lives and has His being. The clothes do not make the man, not even the man of the cloth, and mere form does not make a service, though no worship of God can be devoid of a certain amount of form that is conducive to what Paul calls decency and good order. He also warns that there may be a form of religion that denies its power.

I still smart from a question asked me in a sacristy in Sweden where the clergyman viewed himself in a mirror admiringly, until he could control himself no longer. "But, my dear brother," he explained, "you must admit it's pretty."

My answer was, and is, in the words of another Swedish commentator in regard to the robe Jesus wore at His trial,

> Thy garment is bloodstained,
> Thy spirit doth groan,
> In agony prostrate
> Thou sufferest alone.

No denominations and no organizations have the right to insist that their way of describing Jesus, or robing Him, is the one and only device by which men might come to Him, or learn to know Him. There is altogether too much of such insistence which makes possible the accusation that men are not created in the image of God, but God in the image of men. Any attempt to put the Eternal into vest-pocket size, and deliver Him in a neatly wrapped package to either labor or capital, church or state, monarchies or democracies, favored races or religions, United Nations or disunited Leagues of Nations, is evidence of a God who is precisely like ourselves. He is too small for a God-sized job. Let all God-makers and Jesus-designers take to heart Tennyson's timely and timeless reminder:

> Our little systems have their day;
> They have their day and cease to be;
> They are but broken lights of Thee,
> And Thou, O Lord, art more than they.

Nevertheless, these man-made robes of Jesus are typical of what is always done to the Infinite by us finite, frail, and feeble creatures. The temptations to have Him sign over our papers as a guarantee for our own undertakings beset and often get the best of all of us. In all fairness it should be said that it is a practice not confined to religion alone. From our own history we remember how Lincoln was quoted by the carpetbaggers, whose every plan and purpose was contrary to all that Lincoln embodied and expressed.

St. Francis of Assissi was hardly cold in his grave before his tenet of poverty and renunciation of self was cancelled. Property was acquired and has been accumulated at such rapid rate that the order of St. Francis of Assissi is one of the wealthiest in the world today. Joan of Arc was burned at the stake by the same church that later canonized her and made her a saint.

The protective covering afforded those it never intended to protect by the Fourth and Fifth Amendments to our Constitution is another case in point. Segregationists quote lustily and glibly from the Fourteenth Amendment to have it say the direct opposite from its original intention. Somebody with an eye for business has issued "widow's mite" coins which now go under the hammer for $4.50. Business is business, and whatever gets by and around codes of fair trade is considered legitimate.

One generation slays the prophets, and another turns and twists their teachings, until they are deemed worthy of a monument or a statue in a city square, and pronounced benefactors and friends of man.

To put it mildly, there are some strangely dressed and decorated people on display and exhibit in both church and state, where they are as much out of place as a bomb-throwing anarchist in the White House. Jesus is one of them, followed by a long army of prophets and patriots, martyrs and mighty men of action of whom the world neither was nor is worthy.

By way of contrast, our Lord's own plain, homespun tunic is the one that the soldiers rejected and used as a prize or booty in a dice game. Scriptures describe it as a seamless robe. Countless associations and memories centered around it. There was the woman of Capernaum who said within herself, "If I only touch his garment, I shall be made well."

No doubt little children loved to touch it, and especially to play with its fringes. The same robe was wonderfully and miraculously changed on the Mount of Transfiguration where it became "dazzling white." When the wind blew on the lake of Galilee, Jesus pulled the same robe closer to himself as a means of protection against the elements. On the first Maundy Thursday, Jesus tossed the same robe aside, girded himself with a towel, and began to wash the disciples' feet. From these and more examples that could be quoted we may draw the specific lesson that, whenever and wherever the man Jesus appeared and His robe is mentioned, then and there people were strangely moved and uplifted. That is about as far as I would stress the significance of the robe Jesus wore.

In his well-known book, *The Robe,* Lloyd Douglas insists that no one who ever touched it was ever quite the same. Such a viewpoint borders on the magical and superstitious, from which we need to beseech the good Lord to deliver us. The truth of the matter is that we need not read any such interpretation into it. Yet, from it we may gather the comforting thought that Jesus made the robe so much part of himself that friend and foe alike recognized in it a symbol of hope and help. This is the thought conveyed by the hymn writer when he refers to Jesus as

> The friend of sinners, yet 'tis He
> With garments dyed on Calvary.

Isaiah speaks of a robe so stained with blood and tears that the mind instinctively remembers the simplicity, sincerity, and sacrifice which characterized everything Jesus said and did. Those were the qualities He wore like a monarch's robe, and they remained even after the soldiers had finished their strange chore, which included stripping Him of His garment. Like Him we must remain unwilling to stain the spotless ermine of our royal robes with deed or word or thought of evil. Only a right estimate of our own inherent God-granted dignity and grand possibilities will make us permanently dissatisfied with the low aims and unworthy lives that make no room for an imitation of Christ's simplicity, sincerity, and sacrifice. As a matter of fact such a robe is the only one worth having, for,

"This spotless robe the same appears,
When ruined nature sinks in years:
No age can change its constant hue;
Thy blood preserves it ever new."

The Two Realms

IT WAS EIGHT o'clock in the morning, sacred passion time, when Jesus was brought before Pontius Pilate. Because the enemies of our Lord were scrupulously religious people, and did not wish to defile themselves before eating the passover, they entered not into the praetorium. This meant that the Roman governor and the Savior of the world were by themselves in the judicial chambers and headquarters of justice, where they conducted the strangest question-and-answer period known to man.

Jesus, who both heard and knew what went on among the maddened and maddening crowd outside the courtroom, was highly suspicious of Pilate and for good reason. In answer to his interrogation "Are you the King of the Jews?" He countered with another question "Do you say this of your own accord, or did others say it to you about me?" Instead of giving a direct reply, Pilate introduced an entirely different matter saying "Am I a Jew? Your own nation and the chief priests have handed you over to me; what have you done?"

Although Jesus did not answer the question directly, He defined His kingdom as "not of this world." Pilate was apparently not too concerned about the otherworldly features of our Lord's kingdom, but he was anxious to learn whether or not his strange prisoner considered himself a king. So he repeated his question a second time saying, "So you are a king?" It was then that Jesus answered "You say that I am a king. For this was I born, and for this I have come into the world, to bear witness to the truth. Every one who is of the truth hears my voice."

At this point it becomes rather obvious that the two men were thinking in terms of two entirely different realms or kingdoms. According to His own words and deeds "the King of the Jews" will not push and shove and elbow and shout for living space and recognition, as do the so-called great ones of this world. But He pleads with us today as individuals, as a church, as a nation, and as families, in the same manner as He spoke to Pilate and his contemporaries, to make room for His kingdom, though it is not an earthly one. He gave His own generation and followers an example which remains the same inspiration and force for good yesterday, today, and forever. This is how Peter remembers and describes the life, trial, and death of Jesus: "For to this have you been called, because Christ also suffered for you, leaving you an example, that you should follow in his steps. He committed no sin; no guile was found on his lips. When he was reviled, he did not revile in return; when he suffered, he did not threaten; but he trusted to him who judges justly. He himself bore our sins in his body upon the tree, that we might die to sin and live to righteousness. By his wounds you have been healed. For ye were straying like sheep, but have now returned to the Shepherd and Guardian of your souls."

He was and lived and moved and had His being among us as one that serves. Through all eternity He shall be remembered and revered as Jesus, who "went about doing good." He saved others, himself He could not and cared not to save, if thereby He would lose the purpose of His calling and mission in the world. He washed and cleansed others while himself He could not and cared not to wash free from guilt and stain as long as one soul did in sin and shame remain.

For further comparison and contrast between the two realms, one served by Pilate and the other by Jesus, I wish to cite as evidence the two basins which were used, one by the judge and the other by the prisoner. When after several attempts at face saving, "Pilate saw that he was gaining nothing, but rather that a riot was beginning, he took water and washed his hands before the crowd, saying, 'I am innocent of this righteous man's blood; see to it yourselves.' "

This is the last desperate attempt of a man who had majored in evasiveness all his life to escape responsibility. He had chased with the dogs and run with the hares for so long that he thought he could outsmart everybody, including the King of truth. Until he was brought face to face with Jesus, he had considered himself an expert in the fine and difficult art of carrying water on both shoulders. Now at his wit's end, he resorted to theatrics, washing his hands in full view of the public. His grand strategy of sending Jesus to Herod having ended in complete failure, he calls for the basin of evasion and irresponsibility, "I am innocent of this righteous man's blood; see to it yourselves."

This pathetic and manifestly absurd plea of innocence means that Pilate was dead long before his frame collapsed. He was dead to truth, but alive to cynicism. His conscience had expired long ago, and he heard only the call of opportunism. On the altar of political expediency he had sacrificed the costly and precious gift of integrity, and as a substitute he had accepted the burnt-out ashes of personal ambition to serve and improve himself only. He had lived with falsehood for so long that he believed and followed and loved lying and treachery. "Cowards such as he die many deaths, the valiant but once," and even so their works do follow them.

From Pilate's sorry and disgraceful exhibition of political morality at its lowest and worst, there comes the very valuable and needful lesson that it is possible to defy conscience until it is cowed and crushed. A bit of steel dropped in the compass box will deflect the needle, beat the heavens and wreck the ship.

The most accurate watch becomes speedily worthless as a time-keeper when carried too near a powerful dynamo. On the other hand, when conscience becomes imperial, then life takes on a regal quality, as it did in the case of Jesus, and every faculty of the soul is ennobled and strengthened. The law of love leads to the unfolding of every commendable quality, until the areas of the soul become the garden of the Lord. But as there are no great conquests without mighty convictions, so there are no convictions without an enlightened conscience.

Edna St. Vincent Millay has said the same thing in the often quoted lines, which also suggest the two realms:

The world stands out on either side
No wider than the heart is wide;
Above the world is stretched the sky,—
No higher than the soul is high.
The heart can push the sea and land
Farther away on either hand;
The soul can split the sky in two,
And let the face of God shine through.

That's what Jesus did. Nowhere is this exemplified more clearly than when according to the Passion story, "A dispute also arose among them, which of them was to be regarded as the greatest." "Jesus knowing that the Father had given all things into his hands, and that he had come from God and was going to God, rose from supper, laid aside his garments, and girded himself with a towel. Then he poured water into a basin, and began to wash the disciples' feet, and to wipe them with the towel with which he was girded."

None of the Twelve seemed aware of the basin standing there, waiting for the chance to minister and to show hospitality. All twelve men were too busy debating who was the greatest to take the presence of the water basin in their midst seriously.

Perhaps Peter reasoned within himself that he was the chief and the first ranking disciple. Surely the Master had more elevated service scheduled for him than the menial labor of foot washing, usually reserved for slaves. Andrew had brought Peter, and so slave labor was out of the question for him. James and John had their eyes on the chief seats, and wouldn't think of waiting upon anybody. Judas was more concerned with money than with service. Philip also had a mind good at figures, but was slow in the ability to recognize the true worth of the commonplace. Thomas doubted practically everything except his own doubts. Nathanael was bothered about the good that often is derived from deeds of kindness and mercy. A complete lack of ambition and appreciation so possessed the rest that they feared that, if they did it once, they might start something, and be expected to keep the hated task going. At any rate, nobody did anything, except present demands for recognition and honor.

As usual, Jesus thought of it from an entirely different point of view. He saw not only the dial on the clock of the sacred passion, but the whole works where each part fitly joined together pointed to God's time for action. There was more to the circle than the broken fragment that represented the thirty-three years of anguish He had endured among sinners; "Knowing . . . that he had come forth from God and was going to God . . . he poured water into a basin, and began to wash the disciples' feet." He could have reached for a star, but took a towel instead. He could have lorded it over them, but preferred to serve them, in keeping with His own definition of service, "Whoever would be great among you must be your servant, and whoever would be first among you must be slave of all. For the Son of man also came not to be served, but to serve, and to give his life as a ransom for many."

Here is more than mere definition of terms. It is definitely direction for living in such a way that every word and act shall please both God and men, and serve their highest good. This is radically different from our way of computing values. How insipid our observation alongside of His contribution. "He was a great man, yet He did it," we say. "Although He was great He did it, or in spite of His great fame and name He did it." We ought both to know and to say that because He was great He did it. A great man does great things because of what and who he is, never in spite of it.

Now according to Scriptures Jesus washed the disciples' feet before He instituted the Lord's Supper on Maundy Thursday, the day of the new commandment that as His disciples and followers we should love one another even as He loved us. Interestingly enough, Matthew, Mark, Luke, and the Apostle Paul tell how Jesus in the night when He was betrayed took bread, and when He had given thanks, He broke it and gave it to them saying, "This is my body which is for you. Do this in remembrance of me." In like manner also the cup, after supper saying, "This cup is the new covenant in my blood. Do this, as often as you drink it, in remembrance of me."

John, the disciple whom Jesus loved, has a different point of view, not contradicting but rather complementing and completing the picture of Jesus in all His truth and grace. "I have given you an example"—a visual aid presentation of service. John says nothing about taking the bread and the cup, but he would have us remember that the basin and the towel fill as urgent a need as the bread and the cup. Of course, we ought to eat the sacramental bread and drink the testamental cup, but we ought not neglect the basin and the towel. In Pilate-like fashion we are prone to wash our hands of all responsibility for what happens in our communities, churches, and the world at large. Lady Macbeth tried the same stunt only to cry in the face of frustration and futility, "Out I say, out damned spot." Thousands of others have tried the same trick and have discovered that

> "Not what my hands have done,
> Can save the guilty soul;
> Not what my toiling flesh has borne
> Can make my spirit whole."

So how can we escape if we lose by default the blessings inherent in service rendered for the purpose of keeping man and society spiritually straight and morally pure? Service rendered in Christ's name and because the workman calls Jesus Master shall not go unrewarded, even if the insignia of office is only a lowly basin or a scrub bucket. Said Florence Nightingale, when the romance of nursing the wounded in the Crimean war resulted in a veritable army of volunteers, "The strongest and the best of you will stand by the wash tub." Just so! Let the line for the basin brigade form as a protest against the misuse and perversion still practiced by the Pilates of this world in their feverish attempts to justify and excuse their own sin and guilt.

The realm of self-seeking and self-exoneration is real to all whose ambition it is to follow in the footsteps of Pilate, but the realm of sacramental service is also a reality to all who have the mind which was in Christ Jesus, who though He existed in the form of God, "did not count equality with God a thing to be grasped, but emptied himself, taking the form of a servant, being born in the likeness of men. And being found in human form he humbled himself and became obedient unto death, even death on a cross. Therefore God has highly exalted him and bestowed on him the name which is above every name, that at the name of Jesus every knee should bow, in heaven and on earth and under the earth, and every tongue confess that Jesus Christ is Lord, to the glory of God the Father."

The Two Realists

PREACHERS ARE OFTEN admonished to be practical and realistic. Such advice is offered freely by both proponents and opponents of the Christian faith. But whether the reminder comes from friend or foe, the implication that the Christian religion is impractical and out of touch with reality is identically the same. By the same token, preachers with the down-to-earth approach are told, and even ordered, by the selfsame critics, to stick to the gospel. If I may paraphrase Kipling for a moment, the notion seems to prevail that reality is reality, and Christianity is Christianity, "and never the twain shall meet."

This deplorable divorce between reality and Christianity is definitely the cutting asunder of what God has joined together. Moreover, it is the unashamed confession that the Christian faith has nothing to offer a world that wallows in sin and misery despite the fact that Christians pray, "Thy will be done, on earth as it is in heaven." Furthermore such a division of activity aids and abets the erroneous notion that business is business, art is art, and religion is religion, with some such label as "for external use only" or "dangerous except in small doses." Hence it is often true, as Swinburne complained about a certain preacher, "For tender minds he served up half a Christ." Worst of all, the attempt to keep Christianity away from certain areas and activities is nothing less than a crucifying afresh of the Son of God. For, as Luccock observes with characteristic succinctness and incisiveness, "Jesus was not put to death for saying, 'Behold the flowers of the field, how they grow,' but He was crucified for saying, 'Behold the thieves, how they steal.' " To make matters worse for himself, our Lord included even kings and rulers among thieves and brigands.

For despite His silence when arraigned before King Herod, that was in effect what Jesus said to the sorry clown He had previously referred to as "that fox." If ever silence were golden, it was when Herod questioned our Lord with many words, and in reply He answered the vicious sneak nothing. In a way, this was a personal duel between King Herod and King Jesus, but it was much more than a personal struggle between two men: it was a conflict involving two forces, one of which was physical, the other moral. In fact, it was a visible embodiment of the struggle between good and bad, a clash between heaven and hell fought on this earth. The outcome of that battle found Christianity so inseparably joined with reality that never since has the one been able to live and labor happily and effectively without the other.

Let us, therefore, look at the two chief actors in this divine tragedy, first as men and then as symbols. Take first the king, Herod Antipas. Of all the tyrants who since that day until now have developed the cross, the torture chamber, the guillotine, the salt mine, the death march, the slave labor camp, the purge, the pogrom, the ghetto, the brain wash technique, and liquidation, I doubt that they out-Heroded Herod.

Time would fail me to give an itemized account of the homicidal mania of this inhuman monster, worse by far than any Frankenstein fiction. Suffice it to say that he killed his wife's uncle and forty-five of his followers. All in all, he had 10 wives, and he killed at least one of his mothers-in-law, his sons Aristobulus and Alexander, and three hundred guardsmen who sympathized with Alexander. Next he murdered the second husband of his sister Salome, and the remnants of the great Maccabee family.

Add to all these domestic murders uncounted thousands of others, done for political advantages or from fear or ambition or from sheer bloodthirstiness, and you may realize that Herod's command that all infants two years of age and under in and near Bethlehem be killed was only a minor episode, not even mentioned by Josephus, the historian of those days.

These things are facts, not fiction; they are rooted in reality, and are in no way, shape, or manner, part of an overly active imagination. Sad to say, they are still with us, as Studdert-Kennedy reminds us in a rather realistic fashion,

> Here on earth as the years pass by,
> Centuries piled upon Calvary
> The story of man is but one long line
> Of insults heaped on the plan Divine.
> Murder and misery, rape and war
> Sin like an opening festering sore,
> Oozing its filth through the souls of men,
> Dragging them down to the dust again.
> Children conceived and born in sin,
> Rotten with syphilis, soaked in gin,
> Housed like pigs in their filthy styes
> Cursed from the day they opened their eyes.

Yes, tyrants are still riding high and mighty in practically all areas of life. For example, how can anybody look at the international situation today and deny the reality of King Herod's influence? Being dead, he yet rules, and as evidence he presents long hospital trains loaded with dead and mutilated bodies, nations morally and financially bankrupt, priceless works of art and beauty destroyed beyond repair, and millions of people homeless, naked, thirsty, and starving for a crust of bread. Add to this sordid and shameful picture the ugly disputes between management and labor, the plain man crucified again between the two thieves of dishonest labor leaders on the one hand and the old pilferer inflation on the other.

Then there are class hatreds, racial inequalities, passion, envy, lust, and pride, snobbishness, arrogance, and a superiority complex. On top of all this heap of iniquity are our broken homes and our moral and political corruption. Self-centered living has the cup of fury running over with crime and lust, dishonesty and immorality, alcoholism and the drug habit.

Did I say a moment ago that we would be the losers in any attempt to out-Herod Herod? If ever a man sowed the wind and left his hapless descendants to reap the whirlwind, Herod the king is the man. Faith, hope, and love never entered into the warped and darkened chambers of his mind. Idealism, the soul, the will of God, and the welfare of man were non-existent so far as Herod was concerned, and they are so treated by his followers today. "Let's be realistic," they advise. "The way to power goes through the sea of blood, and the throne of authority is fashioned by bayonets, machine guns, and bombs. You've got to be realistic about it, the only way to get ahead is to let heads roll. Force is the only power in the world, and the only reality, worth knowing and heeding." We even have a name for it, "Real Politik."

Assuredly this is reality, but at its worst, not at its best. The Christian religion that "conquers in dying" makes bold that slums are real, but so are beautiful homes; sewers are real, but so are peacefully flowing rivers; ugliness is real, but so is beauty; lust is real, but so is love; vice is real, but so is virtue; sickness is real, but so is health; death is real, but so is life; dishonesty is real, but so is honesty; falsehood is real, but so is truth; Herod is real, but so is Jesus Christ; the devil is real, but so is God.

Christianity insists that the basement life of society is not all there is to life; there is a higher level, an upper room, a house not made with hands, reserved in the heavens for all who are willing to be redeemed by Jesus Christ, and kept by the power of God. While much realism in literature insists in true Herod fashion that bedrooms and bathrooms are the only real part of a house, and sex the only real purpose of man, Christ would also have us include the chapel, the library, the sun parlor, the living room, and the kitchen so that, whether we eat or drink, it shall all be done to the glory of God.

In all fairness it should be noted and admitted that secularism and materialism are not Christianity's only competitive powers. There is another one that stands at the very opposite end of secularism. For want of a better word we may call it apocalypticism. It affirms and confesses the dynamic and eternal power of the living God; but it does not think or believe that He is present in this world, or that He will have anything to do with a civilization that is sick and sinful and in mortal pain from head to foot.

This view ignores the fact that the Lord God, Maker of heaven and earth, "does not faint or grow weary." It is a view that forgets that God is the greatest materialist of all, and uses material substance to convey spiritual truth. Jesus himself made use of water at His baptism, bread and wine in the institution of the Last Supper, an ordinary boat to cross the lake, a wooden cross upon which, as the Prince of Glory, to die, a rock-hewn grave in which to be buried, and a burning fire and fish at the last breakfast, following His resurrection.

These otherworldly exponents of Christianity also overlook the fact that Jesus accepted and encouraged social responsibility. So He enjoined His followers to cheer the sick, visit the imprisoned, clothe the naked, provide homes for the homeless, bind up the wounds of the broken hearted, serve the cup of cold water to the thirsty, and preach the gospel of God's saving grace to the poor.

The extremes of secularism and of apocalypticism are aberrations and caricatures of the Christian faith. Let all take heart, because God is present in this world and in the life of this civilization, as He has been and will be, world without end. It is our Christian task to bear witness to the truth that the Lord of life and death is not bound or limited by the rise and fall of empires, cultures, and civilizations; it is also our task as Christians to fulfill our calling by serving the needs of this present age. Grounded and rooted in the reality of God's unchanging love at work in an ever-changing world, we must bend every effort, under God, to defeat the Herods of the world whose realism is so naive and childish, and replace it by a reality and power that shall hasten the day when "The kingdom of the world has become the kingdom of our Lord and of his Christ, and he shall reign for ever and ever."

But there is no crown without a cross. The old rugged cross is a towering reminder of the fact that true Christianity comes to grips with things and persons as they are, wherever and whoever they may be. This is illustrated rather aptly by a conversation that took place at an almost completed new church. As a matter of fact, the workmen were fitting the tall slender metal cross to the tower. It was almost evening when they finished and Easter Sunday was right around the corner. Everything seemed to breathe the Spirit of God on this April evening between Good Friday evening and Easter Sunday morning. The cross, etched against the sunset, symbolized both the purpose of the building and the reason for Christ's suffering and death.

"And as Moses lifted up the serpent in the wilderness, so must the Son of man be lifted up, that whoever believes in him may have eternal life." "For God so loved the world that he gave his only Son, that whoever believes in him should not perish but have eternal life." As a matter of fact, the preacher felt a sermon coming when one of the men opined, "Pastor, that cross has to be grounded first thing in the morning, a metal cross like that ungrounded can be dangerous."

What a sermon it was, and what a reminder it has been through the years! The cross of Christ must always be grounded. It must be grounded in the reality of human experience. It dare not remain an isolated theological concept. It must be a vital part of life itself.

Nineteen hundred years ago the redemptive love of God was poured out for all mankind on a cross. Yet the cross is more than a historical event. It was Jesus who said, "If any man would come after me, let him deny himself and take up his cross and follow me." In the words of an old hymn we might ask,

Must Jesus bear the cross alone,
And all the world go free?
No, there's a cross for every one,
And there's a cross for me.

Or as Henry Ward Beecher puts it, "Religion means work, religion means work in a dirty world. Religion means peril; blows given but blows taken as well. Religion means transformation. The world is to be cleaned by somebody and you are not called of God if you are ashamed to scour and scrub."

The Two Rulers

FOR THOSE OF us who feel any interest whatever in ecclesiastical matters, the Christian Year is a source of constant surprise and amazement. As we journey along under the leadership and guidance of our blessed Lord, we are bewildered, just as He was, by the evidence of faith where we least expect it, and by the absence of it where we are prone to take it for granted. This is true already in the Advent season, when the spiritual scene is dominated by a strange uncouth figure, nicknamed John the Baptist, who comes from his austere training school in the desert with the fiery message that men must be prepared and ready to receive their long-awaited Messiah.

The instinctive reaction to a messenger of John the Baptist's caliber is astonishment that the appointed and accepted religious rulers were apparently as unprepared as the people whose spiritual advisers they claimed to be. In other words, God who "at sundry times and in divers manners" had bypassed man-made organizations in the past, did so once more when in the fulness of time His Son was about to be born, with no advance notice or information for the religious rulers. Only a virgin named Mary knew all about it beforehand.

As a matter of fact, the Christmas picture is also remarkable both for what and whom it includes as well as what and whom it excludes. In the closer circle, there is a stable at midnight, some drowsy cattle and sleepy innkeepers, the straw, and the manger in which "sleeps in heavenly peace" the newborn child. Then there are the eager shepherds, who stand on tiptoe to get a good look, and then nod to each other as though some long dormant hope had been fulfilled, robed in flesh. But again the religious leaders are conspicuous by their absence. They are not included, or manifesting any concern whatsoever. In today's parlance, they were not up to date on the latest developments, but woefully behind times, completely ignorant about what was going on in the world.

Strangely enough, the Wise Men must be included in the same category. They, too, arrived late. By the time they had verified and studied the news, it was already common knowledge among the plain people. Lincoln's observation that "God must have loved the common people because He made so many of them" was an established fact even in the days and times of Jesus.

It is part of the record that Jesus himself said substantially the same thing when He prayed saying, "I thank thee, Father, Lord of heaven and earth, that thou hast hidden these things from the wise and understanding and revealed them to babes; yea, Father, for such was thy gracious will." He also said to the chief priests and the Pharisees, in language they understood full well was meant for them and no one else, "The kingdom of God will be taken away from you and given to a nation producing the fruits of it." Again He warned them that when the door had been shut for good and they find themselves outside looking in, no prayers, no sighs and certainly no tears, would alter the situation. "There you will weep and gnash your teeth, when you see Abraham and Isaac and Jacob and all the prophets in the kingdom of God, and you yourselves thrust out."

Those were, and still are, both strong and fateful words. They are brave as regards men, and they are brave as regards God also. Certainly the religious rulers had all the time needed to take them to heart. But they were heard and remembered merely for the case they would build and fortify against Jesus; never once were they considered in the light of literal truth that was to turn with vengeance upon the spiritual aristocrats and autocrats who laid heavy burdens upon others, but would not lift as much as a finger to remove them.

It remained for Palm Sunday and Holy Week, however, to bring into still sharper focus the contrast between Jesus the high priest who can be, and is, touched with the feeling of our infirmities and Caiaphas who so forgot and ignored his office and responsibilities as high priest, that he said to the council, "You know nothing at all; you do not understand that it is expedient for you that one man should die for the people, and that the whole nation should not perish."

Thus the preparations had been laid beforehand for a final showdown between the forces of Jesus and the followers of Caiaphas. Both Jesus and Caiaphas appealed to the masses for permission to rule and guide them in spiritual matters. The contest was brought into the open when on that first Palm Sunday Jesus entered the gates of the Holy City as the Prince of Peace. He came riding upon the colt of an ass, and the people in a moment of jubilation and abandonment of all inhibition imposed by custom and tradition, spread their garments in the way, tore down their palm branches to the tune of "Hosanna! Blessed be he who comes in the name of the Lord!"

Then as He rode amid the shouts and applause of the people, who were almost delirious with delight, He came to a bend in the road from where the city of Jerusalem could be seen. At the sight of the Holy City He burst into a flood of tears. He saw the city as hostile to Him and doomed to destruction. Christ knew that this apparently splendid beginning was really the end for Him.

On numerous occasions in the past He had both foreseen and foretold it all. He knew that He could no more win over thousands of years of prejudice and the arrogant self-satisfaction of that proud city than He could overthrow the great wall encompassing it by pushing against it with His shoulders, no matter what their strength. If more reminders about what awaited Him in the city of Jerusalem were necessary, they were furnished by the religious rulers who commanded Him to restrain His disciples and the people. He answered that, if they were silent, the very stones of the road would speak. It was necessary that He, the Ruler of wind and wave, of meek men and brave men, should enter Jerusalem with a shout of triumph.

Palm Sunday is, therefore, more than the mere beginning of Holy Week, and the day when Jesus entered Jerusalem. The entire week becomes the supreme meeting place between God and men. This is the week for which the centuries had been waiting. Prophets had suffered and perished out of Jerusalem for hundreds of years. Such men of God as Isaiah and Jeremiah had loved, labored, and apparently lost both the cause for which they lived and their lives as a final and generous gesture of devotion to a generation that failed to see the day of visitation and opportunity.

The time for warning had given way to time for action. No longer could the object lesson Jerusalem needed be issued by word of mouth, but by the Word of God incarnate. Mere exhortation would no longer suffice, for the day of demonstration had dawned. Instruction had been replaced by incarnation. The Word had become flesh, and lived and rode and wept among men, as had been foretold.

"He tears, like other men, will shed,
Our sorrows share, and be our aid."

Here was a fact, a force, and a faith no man can elude or escape. This is the victory that overcomes the world, our faith.

Cynical, crafty Caiaphas tried all the tricks he knew to gain the upper hand and keep it there. They included lying and cheating, perjury and such reasonable persuasion as that it is better that one man should die for the people rather than that the whole nation should perish. He was a good talker, and has succeeded since that day until now in deceitfully persuading some people that life is a sort of spiritual supermarket where man shops around, selects his desired and coveted articles on the bargain and barter counter, and leaves strictly alone whatever cramps his style or disagrees with his taste.

It's a powerful argument, Dr. Caiaphas, and as you well know, men swallow it hook, line and sinker. "It is expedient for you that one man should die for the people, and that the whole nation should not perish." But the business of real religion is not to domesticate either God or man, or nationalize them, but to build a bridge across the chasm that keeps God on the outside.

The cross becomes God's way to man, and man's way to God. Christ is the bridge between earth and heaven, and the way that must be trod, if men would ever pass to God. One dying for all means that the life He gave is rich and inclusive enough to become "the life of all the living." In Luther's words, "Christians are to become little Christs to their fellow men." This means that they do more than use strong and dangerous words from the Bible which they have no intention to follow. A friendly critic has likened Christianity to an eagle which people captured, deprived it of its claws, straightened out the beak, and turned it into a tame and talkative crow.

Someone else with a feeling for the ludicrous, put it into cheap poetry at the end of World War II:

Professor A. wants a postwar world where nations will be polite,
But Architect B. wants a postwar world where buildings attain new height.
And Doctor C. wants a postwar world where knowledge has conquered disease,

While Diplomat D. wants a postwar world where everyone aims to please.

Senator X. wants a postwar world where labor and capital kiss,
And Minister Y. wants a postwar world where nothing will go amiss.

Lecturer Z. wants a postwar world where battle banners are furled.

To all of these ideals and lofty aims John Q. the public replies,
"They make me sick, what I want and quick, is simply a postwar world."

All of us are familiar with the cry "to get the boys home" and "back to normalcy," once the high point of a crisis has been reached. We know, too, that the wicked are for their generation and purposes more tenacious and persevering than are "the children of light." There is, however, no bargain basement where peace may be had cheap, or spiritual gains achieved without cost. Christians, of all people, must accept and expect that efforts rather than ease, and plodding in preference to pleasure, are in keeping with the high calling of God in Christ Jesus.

Those who have neither ambition nor imagination to drop more than a mere coin into the wishing well, should not be surprised if the only reward is a splash in the face. It is not expedient that one man dies for the people, or that a certain group of diehards in church and community do all the work, while the majority of people come around once in a great while to see how things are coming along, or how they are doing over at church or school, at City Hall, or in Springfield, or Washington. It is expedient that every life shall have a master, every person a purpose, so that he might be at peace with himself and in communion with God.

Perhaps some of you have read that rather romantic fiction entitled *To Have and to Hold.* The hero has a servant by the name of Diccon, a wild passionate, headstrong ruffian. On a dangerous journey through the Virginia forest the master and the servant have a falling out. The master gives Diccon his dismissal, "Go, I will put up with you no longer. You are no servant of mine." In spite of his dismissal, circumstances force the two angry men to travel on together and a few days later, in a brush with the Indians, Diccon is shot and fatally wounded. As he lies there on the dead leaves, bleeding his sinful life away, his erstwhile master bends over him to hear his last request, "Master, take me back into your service." "Why?" says the master. "Because," comes the answer, "when I face the Lord Jesus I don't want to tell Him that I died a masterless man."

Therein lies a parable to the effect that there is no permanent triumph for the good unless God is in it. Life needs not only a master plan, but a master man.

"Ask ye who this may be?
Christ Jesus, it is He."

Take God out of good, and there is only zero left. Even with God at our side there is the long, agonizing road that stretches endlessly ahead from the city of man to the city of God. John Milton felt the truth when the Puritan Revolution failed in England after a temporary victory. It seemed to him that Paradise had been lost. He wrote then, "Long is the way and hard, that out of hell leads up to life."

The long road is ahead of us all as we struggle for the ideals that make life worth living. It is lined with would-be rulers of Caiaphas' ilk and disposition. Something of the jeers and jibes that were hurled at Jesus even on the day of apparent triumph will have to be borne by all who would valiantly accept the authority of Jesus rather than enjoy the cynicism of Caiaphas. John Henry Jowett describes the cynic as a "disbeliever in the inherent worth of things. He has no confidence in the sincerity of others. He suggests that there is a rotting decay at the heart of every beautiful thing. He cannot look at a flower without talking about the manure at its roots. When others are admiring a lovely deed, he hints at an unclean motive. Even a mother's love is only an animal instinct, a fierce and merely selfish passion at the very heart of her affection. The cynic penetrates the lovely in search of the unlovely and is always sure that he finds it. Whatsoever things are ugly the cynic thinks on these things." It is into such servitude of the evil spirit that Caiaphas, as a religious ruler, calls his followers even today. The sorry spectacle of the church in Soviet Russia, since the days of the Bolshevik revolution in 1917 until now, is just one instance among many of betrayers and deceivers masquerading under the name of religion.

During this Holy Week, as we seek to prepare ourselves for a blessed communion with Him in His Holy Supper this coming Thursday, and as we follow in His train on Good Friday to the place where He was crucified for our sins, may we ever remember that:

> We are living, we are dwelling
> In a grand and awful time,
> In an age on ages telling;
> To be living is sublime . . . .
> Will ye play, then, will ye dally
> With your music and your wine?
> Up! It is Jehovah's rally!
> God's own arm hath need of thine.
>
> Alexander C. Coxe

The Two Rites

SOME THREE THOUSAND years ago, a colony of Hebrew nomad tribes were slaves in Egypt. Then as now, the feelings between the Israelites and the Egyptians were most unfriendly, hateful, and bitter. The Pharoahs were hard and cruel taskmasters, who knew how to make the serfdom of their despised subjects most intolerable and miserable.

This state of affairs continued for approximately four hundred years. During all this time the groans and prayers of the proud Jewish people increased, but seemingly to no avail. There was no help forthcoming from either God or man. As the chances for freedom diminished, hatred and animosity deepened.

We are still paying the price for the calculated malevolence set in motion in the land of Egypt more than thirty centuries ago. For a realistic estimate of the high cost of hating, the crisis in the Middle East has an answer that, like the sands along the sea shore, or the stars in the heavens above, cannot be computed by the mind of man.

We know this, however, that freedom from slavery does not mean freedom from hatred of former tyrants and oppressors. Both modern and ancient subject peoples have had the chains of bondage removed, only to find themselves imprisoned by a fanatical desire for revenge and retaliation. Time does not necessarily heal all wounds. The Hebrew people illustrate this sad fact most perfectly. As their attitude towards their taskmasters was in the beginning, so it is today, and will continue to be until the end of time, unless there is brought about a change of heart and disposition that will let bygones be bygones.

For physical deliverance came to the sorely tried Hebrews in a night long ago, when they were literally "saved by the blood of the lamb." Each Hebrew family was instructed to kill a lamb, and take the blood of that lamb and strike it on the door posts of the house; then in great haste, with staff in hand, dressed for the journey, they were to eat the roast shank of the lamb with bitter herbs, with unleavened bread, all ready to start and go places "to a land flowing with milk and honey."

That night the angel of death came to Egypt, and whenever that angel saw the lintels of the door streaked with the lamb's blood, he passed by that house. All through the rest of Egypt, outside the slave quarters, there was not a house spared. Everywhere, except among the Hebrews, there was mourning and great lamentation. The slaves were jubilant, however, for the day of redemption and emancipation had arrived at long last! This is the deathless story of the Passover. It is a story remembered and rehearsed to this day in word and sign at every Seder supper. The Pascal Lamb is the abiding symbol of escape from physical bondage, and as such it is the oldest and most significant festival in history.

Paradoxically enough, however, the Feast of the Passover is an occasion when even the devout and the faithful love to seem to be what they are not. The decencies and the deceits of life are strangely present in the passover observance, where from the same mouth is apt to come forth blessing and cursing. St. James' reminder has special significance in the rite of the Passover, where the same tongue is used both to bless the Lord and Father who freed them long ago, but also to indict and condemn men long since dead and their descendants for conditions God himself rectified some three thousand years ago in the most dramatic manner possible. Much has been said and written about the value of this type of religious education where fathers:

"Let children learn the mighty deeds
Which God performed of old,
Which in our youngest years we saw,
And which our fathers told.
Our lips shall tell them to our sons,
And they again to theirs
That generations yet unborn,
May teach them to their heirs."

Now, of course, it all depends on what fathers are teaching their heirs. Many mighty deeds have to do with violence and bloodshed, or in Kipling's words:

Such boastings as the Gentiles do
Or lesser breeds without the law.

To perpetuate the tale of cruelty committed by people who lived in the pre-Christian era is a questionable practice indeed. So is the never-ending agitation about Alsace Lorraine, the Saar region, and Sudeten land, which has cost more blood and tears than we can possibly imagine or think.

In our own country there was the Civil War almost a century ago. To all outward, legal, and military appearances it was settled and so signed on the dotted line. Yet, it is still being fought in classrooms and living rooms in many sections of our land where "children learn the mighty deeds" of a past that for all practical and spiritual purposes ought to be forgotten and buried in the sea of oblivion. Much of what comes to us in religious and patriotic guise is of the quality described on the memorial plaque at Concord bridge, Massachusetts,

They came three thousand miles and died
To keep the past upon its throne,
Beyond the farthest ocean tide
The English mother made her moan.

There is more to living and education than merely to keep a dead past upon its throne. Our national holidays should not be occasions for tirades against foes located in a dead past. In the First Letter to the Corinthians there is a suggested remedy "Cleanse out the old leaven that ye may be fresh dough, as you really are unleavened. For Christ, our paschal lamb, has been sacrificed. Let us, therefore, celebrate the festival, not with the old leaven, the leaven of malice and evil, but with the unleavened bread of sincerity and truth."

"Christ, our paschal lamb, has been sacrificed." One of the collects for Easter Sunday has this prayer, "Almighty and eternal God, Thou Who didst deliver Thy people out of Egypt by the hand of Thy servant Moses, and didst command them to observe the Passover and eat the paschal lamb, bring us also, O heavenly Father, out of the spiritual Egypt, and make us partakers of the true Paschal Lamb, Jesus Christ, our Lord . . ."

Consider also how in the communion liturgy we acknowledge Christ as "our Paschal Lamb, offered for us, the innocent Lamb of God that taketh away the sin of the world. As He hath conquered death, is risen again, and liveth for evermore, even so all they who put their trust in Him shall through Him be victorious over sin and death, and inherit eternal life. And in order that we may keep in remembrance His unspeakable mercy, He hath instituted His Holy Supper."

The setting of the paschal sacrifice, the words reminiscent of the pouring out of blood on the altar by Moses as a sign of the covenant, the literal character of the words of institution themselves, all indicate a new sacrifice, a "new testament" in His blood. This new sacrifice, which Christ instituted in the night in which He was betrayed, He commanded His followers to continue in the memory of His passion; with quiet and simple majesty He took bread, broke it and gave it to them saying, "Take, eat; this is my body, which is given for you; this do in remembrance of me. After the same manner also when he had supped he took the cup and when he had given thanks, he gave it to them saying, 'Drink ye all of it; this cup is the New Testament in my blood, which is shed for you and for many for the remission of sins, this do, as oft as ye drink it in remembrance of me.' "

Our blessed Lord knows our needs. We need mercy for we have been weak. We need grace for we must be strong. Consequently, in the words of the psalmist, "He has caused his wonderful works to be remembered; the Lord is merciful and gracious. He provides food for those who fear him." As a merciful Lord, He has worked a wonderful work; He gave His life for us on the cross, the sign of mercy and redemption. A gracious Lord, He has given us a living remembrance of His mercy in the Sacrament of the Altar. Christ, our Passover, is sacrificed for us, and as often as we eat the bread and drink the cup, we show the Lord's death until He comes.

By whatever name we may call it, be it the Mass or the Eucharist, the Lord's Supper or the Divine Liturgy, or Holy Communion or Sacrament of the Altar, or whatever we may believe about it, or however we may receive it, standing up, sitting down, or kneeling, we all do it because He has commanded us to do it saying, "This do in remembrance of me." Jesus gave himself that we might be set at liberty from the forces that would enslave us. The most tyrannical force of all is self-servitude. He died for us that we might live, no longer for ourselves, but for Him who for our sakes died.

At the Lord's table there is no room for arguments as to who is the greatest, or accusations as to who killed Jesus. Constant reference to the Jewish people as the chief and lone perpetrators of the crime of the ages does not make for better Jewish-Christian relations, nor does it make us better Christians. Suffice it to say that Jesus died to gather together the children of God that were scattered abroad. As all have equal benefits from His atoning death, so all are equally guilty in bringing it about. "He is the expiation for our sins, and not for ours only but also for the sins of the whole world."

"There was no other good enough
To pay the price of sin;
He only could unlock the gate
Of heaven, and let us in."

In addition, there are among Christians disputed areas and forbidden territories corresponding to the Egypt-Israel dispute, the Saar region argument, the Alsace Lorraine Struggle, the Sudeten land problem, and the regional divisions confronting us in the world of politics and geography. We are a divided body, contrary to the intentions and prayers of Jesus. The decencies and deceits of life are present not only in the Passover observance, but equally so in the observance of the rite of Holy Communion. No one has monopoly on God or the patent on the Lord's Supper, or exclusive access to His virtue and grace.

For our sakes He died and rose again. This love of God which He tried to tell us by word and work is not just one mad dash of an impetuous God into the world to save one lost generation or sect or denomination. It is the abiding attitude of the Creator toward His creatures, that not one of them shall perish, lost in shades of night. The liberty He has secured for us is not merely the happiest, highest or most satisfactory way you and I can spend our allotted life span here. It is the very guarantee of life in the everlasting realms and mansions of glory. Therefore, as we commemorate the death of Christ in this feast of the cross, we pray that we may dwell with Him forever as partakers of the Great Supper in heaven.

The Two Revolutionists

HATE IS A very ugly word, conceived in malice, and dedicated to the proposition that men are enemies. It belongs in the same family and household as detest, abhor, abominate, and loathe. All of them are ugly words describing the meanest condition of the human heart. Were we to gather data concerning its usage in everyday speech, we should be happily surprised, I think, to discover how infrequently it is put into circulation, either by us, or among us. Even people who habitually are apt to be careless with their words carefully avoid broadcasting their hatreds. And people who think before they speak are reluctant to confess their animosity toward other fellow beings.

It is only when we are provoked to excessive anger, or when under great mental strain or physical pain, that such words as hate, loathe, detest, and abhor, are given free and unbridled expression. As an illustration we need only remind ourselves that, great as are the tensions in wartime, there was nevertheless a wave of public disapproval when, at the height of the last war, an American general opined that it was our business as a nation "to learn to hate, hate, hate, with every fibre of our being." Though the advice was offered at a time when enemies threatened, mostly with inflammatory speeches, most people evidenced a rather remarkable restraint in the use of invectives. So on the surface of things, at any rate, the familiar prayer seems singularly successful.

Lord, set a seal upon my lips,
For this I pray,
And guard me, keep me, use me, Lord,
Just for today.

That, however, is mostly an exterior appearance. Most of us recognize this sad fact at once. Courtesy and affability are often only skin deep, while inwardly there are all manners and forms of evil. Jesus who, we are told, "knew what was in man," also expressed this unpleasant fact in His customary forthright manner, "Woe to you scribes and Pharisees, hypocrites! for you tithe mint and dill and cummin, and have neglected the weightier matters of the law, justice and mercy and faith; these you ought to have done, without neglecting the others. You blind guides, straining out a gnat and swallowing a camel.

"Woe to you, scribes and Pharisees, hypocrites! for you cleanse the outside of the cup and of the plate, but inside they are full of extortion and rapacity. You blind Pharisee! first cleanse the inside of the cup and of the plate, that the outside also may be clean.

"Woe to you, scribes and Pharisees, hypocrites! for you are like whitewashed tombs, which outwardly appear beautiful, but within they are full of dead men's bones and all uncleanness. So you also outwardly appear righteous to men, but within you are full of hypocrisy and iniquity.

"Woe to you, scribes and Pharisees, hypocrites! for you build the tombs of the prophets and adorn the monuments of the righteous, saying, 'If we had lived in the days of our fathers, we would not have taken part with them in shedding the blood of the prophets.' Thus you witness against yourselves, that you are sons of those who murdered the prophets. Fill up, then, the measure of your fathers. You serpents, you brood of vipers, how are you to escape being sentenced to hell?"

No one will deny that these are unusually strong, sharp, and piercing words, which indicate that Jesus had not come merely to shovel smoke. One might even be inclined to regard them as wasted, for though Jesus rebelled against behavior and attitude manifestly insincere and deceitful, His protests only made things worse instead of better for himself. He was definitely not the kind of person who never has any enemies, and is forgotten completely three days after his funeral. For in His contacts with the religious leaders Jesus was met with customary deference at first. As the cleavage became more apparent, Jesus charged openly that, though they treated Him with nothing more serious than aloofness and suspicion, He was well aware of their intention to kill Him. Their only reply was the enraged outcry, "Who's trying to kill you? When you talk like that we know you have a demon."

But He knew from the first what was taking place in the souls of men, for even in His farewell discourse, in the night when He was betrayed, He warns His followers, saying, "If the world hates you, you know that it has hated me before it hated you." He even quotes a passage from their law to show how real, and yet how unfounded, their hatred of Him was, "They hated me without a cause."

Now it would be comparatively easy to dismiss Jesus as a man gone mad, a psychopath, and a mentally deranged individual, even as both His family and His foes did on a number of occasions, were it not for the important fact that we know how tragically correct Jesus was. This is Good Friday, the day of infamy that will live as the day when maddened men demanded that Barabbas, a robber, should be released to them, and Jesus destroyed.

In vain did Pilate seek to change the minds of the infuriated mob. But according to three of the gospel writers, "They all cried out together, 'Away with this man, and release to us Barabbas'—a man who had been thrown into prison for an insurrection started in the city, and for murder. Pilate addressed them once more, desiring to release Jesus; but they shouted out, 'Crucify, crucify him!' A third time he said to them, 'Why, what evil has he done? I have found in him no crime deserving death; I will therefore chastise him and release him.' But they were urgent, demanding with loud cries that he should be crucified. And their voices prevailed. So Pilate gave sentence that their demand should be granted. He released the man who had been thrown into prison for insurrection and murder, whom they asked for; but Jesus he delivered up to their will."

Superficially speaking, the procedure had all the earmarks of democracy and free election. Pilate made his decision because the people had spoken. Their will was respected. Their desire was granted. They loved darkness as it was embodied in the person of Barabbas, and they hated the light as it was personalized in Jesus Christ. Both Barabbas and Jesus had this in common, that they rebelled against things as they were. They were revolutionists.

Barabbas appealed to national grievances. Nationalism is a powerful weapon in the hands of the unscrupulous. The rabble rouser can accomplish much destruction and add immeasurably to the world's cup of woe by appealing to national interests. Within our own memory we have seen Hitler's boasting come true with verbal accuracy, "By a clever and skillful use of propaganda it is possible to make men believe that black is white and white black, and the blackest hell look like Paradise." Was Hitler taking a lesson from the notebook of Barabbas when he spoke and acted out those seemingly impossible words? Are national and international affairs conducted according to the Barabbas—or the Jesus-approach to life? Is killing, rape, and murder the solution to the world's ills? It would seem so, at least at first sight, for how often is not Barabbas elected the mayor of the city, the representative, or the senator, and Jesus

Christ crucified. The power of the underworld reaches into the courts of justice, and thwarts the punishment of those who have done evil. Is constituted authority carrying the sword in vain? Are people voting their Christian convictions in a community that spends one and a half million dollars annually on the liquor traffic, and turns down a referendum that calls for $15,000 for a recreational program in behalf of its children?

Is acid throwing and the blinding of those who stand like islands of honesty in the swamplands of corruption the will of the people and, if so, are they right when they surrender to hoodlums the management of society? How much longer must we wait, O Lord, before we shall realize that it is the number of square people, not the number of square miles, that makes a country great? People, not institutions, must be changed first. What is needed is not a lynching party for someone else but a surgical operation on ourselves, though a lynching party, except for the victim, is much more fun, if one may judge from the chorus of those who demand that goodness be placed on the scaffold and wrong upon the throne.

What's the cause of this perverted state of affairs? According to our Lord's own words, there is no cause, that is, there is no rational explanations for it, except that we, *the people,* don't know what we are doing when we so hate the Prince of Life that we demand His death, and so love Barabbas with all his violence, bloodshed, and agitation, that we demand and obtain his release.

Herein is the great danger to democracy and free government. The voice of the people is not always the voice of God, as Walter Lippman has so well stated it. What happened on that original Good Friday happens repeatedly, and to our own irretrievable loss. No society can long endure, if constantly led by leaders of the Barabbas ilk, even though they are elected in purportedly free and open elections. Love is so strong, and God so kind in dealing with us in mercy, that society can afford once in awhile to have charlatans, fools, or misfits in positions of power. However, to have them in the seat of the mighty always is to court disaster. Meddlesome mediocrities do make our confusion worse confounded.

A native African, Mabel Imouklade Julaso, has expressed it in these memorable words, "Here we stand, infants overblown, poised between two civilizations, finding the balance irksome, itching for something to happen to tip us one way or the other, groping in the dark for a helping hand, and finding none. I am tired, O my God, I am tired, I am tired of hanging in the middle way, but where can I go?"

In these lines is described not only the conflict in Africa, but what's more, the struggle of every human heart. Where can I go? It is easy enough to answer:

"Come to the Saviour, make no delay;
Here in His Word He's shown us the way;
Here in our midst He's standing today,
Tenderly saying, 'come!' "

From the Word of God we learn that "The Spirit and the Bride say, 'Come.' And let him who hears say, 'Come.' And let him who is thirsty come, let him who desires take the water of life without price."

Moreover, from the Lutheran World Federation came this statement in preparation for the Minneapolis convention in August 1957. "The freedom which Christ has achieved we receive through the Word and the Sacraments. When the Gospel is preached, Christ Himself is present to redeem us from the slavery of sin and death, and to make us a member of His body. Because we now belong to Him, He lets His righteousness now belong to us. The entire purpose of Word and Sacraments is to bring to us this freedom. This is the point at which we should start when we seek the unity of the church . . . Christ, and Christ alone, sets free and unites."

"Them's good words," as the slave says in *Uncle Tom's Cabin,* when for the first time he hears "Come unto me," and then asks suspiciously, "But who says them?"

There lies the rub! The words come from us whose advance for Christ has not included a sufficient advance in faith and fellowship to make it possible for us as Christians to meet unitedly at the Lord's table and in the Lord's house. So far we have failed to find the new and better dimension of insight and understanding which, when it comes, will usher in the religion of brotherhood. In the small world in which we are now living, its vast distances abolished by the magic of science, the races of men are drawn closer and closer together, and rancor runs rife.

In the British Commonwealth this problem is widely distributed, as the Suez Canal and recurring Middle East crises attest so vividly; but in America it is right at our doors, with many both Christians and non-Christians terming it insoluble. The Indian poet Rabindranath Tagore put the matter pointedly many years ago when he asked, "Do you really think that as long as America has such racial prejudice it has any Christianity to export?"

This question, asked more than a quarter of a century ago, assumes special relevance today when nationalism is on the march among the have-not nations of the world, and missionaries, educators, and business men are being expelled and denied entry because India belongs to the Indians, Japan to the Japanese, Africa to the Africans, Asia to the Asiatics, and China to the Chinese—all preferably to the Communists whose gospel of hate, sedition, and uprising is the reincarnation of Barabbas the robber, who gained his freedom at the very moment Christ lost His. Barabbas never quite knew what to make of it.

Neither do we seem to understand that if the old hurts and heartaches of the world are to be healed; if there is to be love where there is now hate; if the shadow of war on both military and commercial battlefields is to be lifted from the life of man; if humanity is to be led towards a more just and a more merciful social order; if the gospel is to be sent into all the corners of the world, we must hear and heed the commandment given us by John the beloved disciple, that "he who loves God should love his brother also." Let us love, then, but not as Barabbas who loved to threaten with word and sword those who stood in the way of his dream of national and individual liberty.

What hideous crimes have not been committed, and still are committed, in the name of liberty—and that not only in totalitarian countries! John Philpot Curran said as far back as 1790: "It is the common fate of the indolent to see their rights become a prey to the active. The condition upon which God hath given liberty to man is eternal vigilance, which condition if he break, servitude is at once the consequence of his crime, and the punishment of his guilt."

Thus we may learn from Barabbas that he, too, is good for something, even if it be to serve as a bad example, whom we must not imitate but rather remember as an illustration of what one of Henric Ibsen's characters expresses so unforgettably, "Our great loss is that we have not loved the highest." Barabbas represents all those lovers of liberty in all walks of life who want what they want on their own terms. Never mind what God says or how it affects their fellow men. Such an unworthy type is still among us. We see him on the street, about the church, and sometimes—in the mirror!

Jesus' approach to life is also revolutionary, but pursued with entirely different means, and with other goals in view than those of Barabbas. It can be summed up in the words of an old-fashioned rhyme:

Baptized of John, the Gospel of fulfilled righteousness He proclaimed,

Then He cast demons out, restored the dead and maimed,

Defied the scribes, and raised the ruler's child;
Stilled the storm, though fierce was the billow wild.
Men's hearts with truth He cleared, their eyes with sight;
Betrayed, against the world upheld His right;
And dying, of His booty death beguiled.
This was no meek and gentle Jesus mild,
Rather it was He whom winds and waves obey
And who o'er hearts and souls does have the final say.

If this is not revolutionary, what is? Men can be born anew, and become heirs of God and joint heirs with Jesus Christ.

"This is our faith tremendous,
Our reason who shall scorn,
That in the name of Jesus,
The world shall be reborn."

The Two Revolts

PRESSED INTO THREE short statements in the Nicene creed is the story of "the two revolts": Christ "was crucified also for us under Pontius Pilate. He suffered and was buried; And the third day He rose again, according to the Scriptures."

Additional details, furnished by all the Evangelists, are to the effect that our Lord was put to death by men who were in open revolt against His announced plan and purpose to save them from sin and death. With the exception of prophets and seers, men were deaf, dumb, and blind concerning the real issues facing them. And even with due regard for the clairvoyance of sages and wise men, it is still true that none has seen more clearly than Jesus how great is the darkness in the world when men dwell in the shadows of fear and suspicion.

The world into which He came preaching and healing was a cruel and divided world; it was, and still is, a world of master and servant, of tyrant and slave, of greed for power, lust, and evil. Men were divided against their neighbors, leaders against their followers, kings against their subjects, nations against nations. Evil certainly was in the ascendancy, becoming more oppressive every day.

Having said that, however, we do well to remember the other side of the story. We must beware, as Ogden Nash warns us, of "one-way thinking on a two-way street." Jesus was not a God during office hours only, concerned merely with reports, graphs, and diagrams as they were prepared for Him by men in the field. He saw with His own eyes that goodness could be depended upon to stage a comeback, if given a chance. From personal contacts and observations, He was convinced that there were people who had a keen hunger and thirst after righteousness. So He decided to help them in every way possible. "Greater love has no man than this, that a man lays down his life for his friends."

In the words of a Sunday school student, "Jesus saw a lot of good in the world, and He didn't like the way it was being pushed around. Someone had to take the rap and Jesus did."

His enemies complained, and they still do, that His teaching about brotherly love was a revolutionary doctrine. It was a hard saying, and they did not intend to follow it. When He besought them to love their enemies, to do good to all that did evil to them, to be kind, merciful and helpful one to another, to walk the second mile, to give to him that asks, and to imitate their Father in heaven, they agreed among themselves that such a fellow should be put away permanently.

So they killed Him, and He accepted death on the cross. "Like a lamb that is led to the slaughter, and like a sheep that before its shearers is dumb, so he opened not his mouth. By oppression and judgment he was taken away" according to the time-honored principle, "Might makes right." "And they made his grave with the wicked and with a rich man in his death, although he had done no violence, and there was no deceit in his mouth."

They killed Him, thinking that thereby they would slay both Him and His ideas. As long as there is life, they reasoned, there is always the chance for trouble, even though He has shown no inclination to defend himself with either sword or fist. Nevertheless, better be safe than sorry. Dead men tell no tales. So they killed Him, for death was the strongest thing they knew. When a man is dead there is nothing else left but to bury him, though they took the additional and unusual precaution of making the grave safe by placing the government seal at the entrance to the tomb, and Roman guards to protect it. Pilate's parting advice, "Make it as sure as you can," indicates that with the God-man Jesus in His grave all is still far from well.

For, wonder of all wonders, on the third day He rose again, and both He and the things He taught have spread until Phillips Brooks' Easter hymn becomes a literal statement of fact:

Tomb thou shalt not hold Him longer,
Death is strong, but Life is stronger,
Stronger than the dark, the light;
Stronger than the wrong, the right;
Faith and Hope triumphant say
Christ will rise on Easter Day.

The very same conviction is stated in Charles Rann Kennedy's play "The Terrible Meek" where the captain who gave the crucifixion order on Good Friday says: "Life is a terrible, a wonderful thing. You can't kill it. All the soldiers in the world with all their hate, can't kill it. It comes back. It can't die. It rises again."

And later: "He's alive. I can't kill Him. All the empires can't kill Him. How shall hate destroy the power that rules the earth?"

That, my friends, is God's revolt. It is God striking back at puny man who stands there like the historic fly on the chariot wheel, exclaiming, "See what dust I am stirring up." We saw them last week confronting each other: God with that look of eternal compassion in His eyes, and with a message of everlasting mercy, "I would but ye would not. However, if this is what you want, proceed. Kill the Prince of Life, but I warn you in advance 'Thus far shall you come, and no farther, and here shall your proud waves be stayed.'" And there is man with a clenched fist, gnashing his teeth, with the marks of Cain on his face, and murder in his heart. What a sad, "has been" he has turned out to be, this crown of creation! Lord Byron's confession comes to mind:

> My days are in the yellow leaf;
> The flowers and fruits of love are gone;
> The worm, the canker, and the grief,
> Are mine alone!

"No," says God, "they are mine also. We'll bear them together to dark Calvary. I have made you a little lower than the angels, and crowned you with dominion and power. Don't think for a moment that I will leave you in the dust, an unhappy crown prince with never a chance to become king. I am so certain of life's victory over death that for your sake I am willing to give myself completely to the bruised, unpopular principles of a reconciling love 'that conquers in dying.' When the task is finished, and the resurrection on the third day is an accomplished fact, you will find death swallowed up in victory. I will take life out of death. Like a tree, he who believes in me may have his autumn, when he is stripped of foliage and other embellishment, but he will also have his spring. I am the resurrection and the life. I am the first and the last, the beginning and the end, and I have the key to death and hell."

So the sorrow of Good Friday is swallowed up in the joy of Easter Sunday. True to His clearly stated promise to lay down His life and take it up again, the Savior of the world has not waited for an inscription to be placed upon the tomb. An angel announces His epitaph, the strangest one ever composed and recorded, "He has risen, he is not here; see the place where they laid him."

The sign which appeared in a cemetery sometime ago was literally true in His case, "Temporary entrance while road is under construction." Death is still a temporary arrangement, despite the old proverb which avers: "Only the grave digger's work is permanent." No proverbs or clever sayings can divert our attention from the transitory aspects of the old, old-fashioned death. With Dickens we cry triumphantly "thank God for the older fashion yet of immortality."

The soul rises above death because Christ has made it glorious and triumphant. Love defies it. Faith in God conquers it. Small wonder that the song writer has included in "The Holy City" the moving exhortation

> Jerusalem, Jerusalem,
> Sing for the night is o'er.

By the transcendent miracle of His resurrection, Christ triumphed over sin and death, gave the lie to His enemies, and proved beyond dispute that neither the gates of death, nor the tomb's dark portal could hold Him as a mortal. "This is the day which the Lord has made; let us rejoice and be glad in it." For this is the day when fulfillment is given to the dreams, the aspirations, and the hopes which we cherish, that eventually mankind can triumph over all sorrow; that as we have suffered with Christ so shall we also be glorified with Him; that our hearts can truly rejoice because our joy no man shall take from us. He is faithful who promised, "Because I live, you will live also."

The death of Christ on the cross and His resurrection from the tomb is God's never-changing formula for the triumph of good over evil, of truth over falsehood, of justice over iniquity, of love over hatred, and of peace over war. By the power of "Love divine, all love excelling" Jesus faced the worst in our behalf, and found the best that ever entered the mind of man, namely, the power of an endless life. It is not a prophecy, but a possession: God is here; eternity is now. Death is nothing to the soul. The dark valley of the shadow of death has become in Christ only a dark room in which life changes its robe of flesh, and marches on, nay wings its flight to realms of day.

As believers in the resurrection miracle, we must, and do,

take issue with the late Fred Allen's mournful philosophy, "Life is a long walk down a dark corridor that grows darker, the nearer one comes to the end." On the contrary, Jesus transfigures, even here and now, all "our fleshly dress with bright shoots of everlastingness." When we know the power of His resurrection, all doors are open, and the great aspirations of the heart take wings, until it becomes the realest thing in the world that to know God in Jesus Christ is life everlasting.

Society itself is held together by those insights and aspirations which issue from the power of an endless life. Liberty, love, and the lordship of Jesus are so definitely and decisively part of eternal life that without them customs are cobwebs and laws mere ropes of sand. It is significant that toward the end of his life Dostoevski, the great Russian novelist, divided the race into two classes, those who know the eternal life and those who do not. The fate of civilization, he added, will rest with those who are citizens of eternity.

Thus the Easter reality has become the creative and constructive force of humanity, and when it is lost society becomes a pigsty. Neither position nor education will suffice as substitute for the Easter life of God in the soul. Souls who have suffered the loss of such a faith are found in penthouses as well as in slums, in universities as well as in homes and offices, and are of all men most pitiable. It is in Him, "the Lord of all good life," that we must find the inspiration for the abundant life, the life that is life indeed, whether for individual or group living.

Only recently have physicians and psychologists come to the conclusion that subconscious health cannot be obtained in one who has lost faith in life everlasting. Apart from it, the noblest powers of the soul are inhibited, and the finest instincts are frustrated. Life for all of us grows in dignity, worth, and meaning, only if and when it draws sustenance and support from the resurrection reality.

In the fellowship of Christ's suffering, and in the power of His resurrection, a man is able to stand up like a tower, four-square to all the winds of the world and all the waves of "life's wild, restless sea." It becomes a tie which unites us with those nearest to us, lengthening until it becomes a golden chord, binding us to all humanity, including those whom we have loved and lost awhile. It is a bond of perfection and peace that makes us feel again and anew the clasp of a hand that is still, and a voice we heard and loved in days that come not back here, but are nonetheless a foretaste of what will be reclaimed, never to be taken from us in the hereafter.

In the words of Robert Louis Stevenson, "Quiet minds cannot be perplexed or frightened any more, but go on in fortune and misfortune like the ticking of a clock in a thunderstorm."

Whatever befalls, and regardless of external circumstances, there is an all-sustaining, undefeatable melody, even in "the hour that darkest seemeth" that "Life is ever lord of death, And love can never lose its own." Hence we confess and pray:

"Safe in the care of heavenly powers
The good we dreamed, but might not do,
Lost beauty magically new,
Shall spring as surely as the flowers
When mid the sobbing of the rain,
The heart of April beats again.

"Celestial spirit that doth roll
The heart's sepulchral stone away,
Be this our resurrection day,
The singing Easter of the soul:
O gentle Master of the Wise,
Teach me to say, I will arise."

"I take, O cross, thy shadow
  For my abiding-place:
I ask no other sunshine than
  The sunshine of His face;
Content to let the world go by,
  To know no gain nor loss;
My sinful self my only shame,
  My glory all, the cross."

"I know that my Redeemer lives!
What comfort this sweet sentence gives!
He lives, He lives, who once was dead,
He lives, my everliving Head."

Date Due
